BASED ON A TRUE STORY

A PUPPY CALLED
DEZ

JOHN TOVEY

WITH
VERONICA CLARK

DINO

Published by Dino Books,
an imprint of John Blake Publishing Ltd,
3 Bramber Court, 2 Bramber Road,
London W14 9PB, England

www.johnblakebooks.com

www.facebook.com/johnblakebooks ⓕ
twitter.com/jblakebooks ⓣ

This edition published in paperback in 2015

ISBN: 978 1 78418 423 0

British Library Cataloguing-in-Publication Data:

A catalogue record for this book is available from the British Library.

Design by www.envydesign.co.uk

Printed in Great Britain by CPI Group (UK) Ltd

1 3 5 7 9 10 8 6 4 2

Papers used by John Blake Publishing are natural, recyclable
products made from wood grown in sustainable forests.
The manufacturing processes conform to the
environmental regulations of the country of origin.

Every attempt has been made to contact the relevant copyright-holders,
but some were unobtainable. We would be grateful if the appropriate
people could contact us.

To Monica, a true friend. Thanks for everything.

CONTENTS

CHAPTER 1

ODD ONE OUT

A paw shoved hard against my back. It felt so rough and sudden that it woke me from my sleep.

'Come on, fat bum, get up!'

'What? Is it breakfast time already?' I yawned, rubbing the sleep from my eyes.

'Is that all you ever think about – food?'

I blinked and tried to focus on the golden figure standing in front of me. Two huge brown eyes glared down. It was Violet, my youngest and meanest sister.

'Shift! You're lying in the middle of the floor again and we haven't got enough room to play,' she hissed, giving me a quick puppy nip on my shoulder.

'Ouch!' I squeaked, although it didn't stop her because whatever Violet wanted, she got.

'Have I missed it then?' I asked, clambering to my feet.

'Missed *what*?'

'Breakfast?'

Violet rolled her eyes towards the ceiling.

'No, you fat bat!' she said, flicking a claw against one of my enormous black ears, dangling either side of my head. 'They're just bringing it over now, but you'd better keep your big snout out of my bowl,' she added, eyes narrowing, 'otherwise there'll be trouble.'

'Oh, I *will*! I only ever eat leftovers,' I insisted.

Only Violet wasn't listening. She'd flounced off with her tail sticking up in the air.

'I don't know where we got him from, he looks nothing like us,' she sniffed to the rest of the litter of puppies – my family.

Huge tears welled at the back of my eyes. Willing them to go away, I tried not to cry because I knew Violet was right – I looked nothing like my sisters and brothers. I was a tall Labrador, with ears that were much too big for my head and shiny black fur, but the rest of the litter were fluffy and golden. Mum told me I looked different because I was special.

'One day, you'll achieve great things. Just you wait and see,' she insisted.

But I didn't want to be different; I wanted to be like the others. I was the second-eldest boy in a litter of guide-dog puppies. We lived at the National Breeding Centre in Bishop's Tachbrook, Warwickshire, where all guide-dog pups begin their lives. One day, we hoped we'd grow up to become proper guide dogs because they were the most important dogs of all. But first we had to study hard and pass loads of difficult exams. Only then would we be allowed to become fully trained guide dogs, and the eyes of a blind or partially sighted person. We'd help them cross the road safely, and walk down the street without tripping up. In short, we'd become their best friend. Everyone needs a best friend, but right then, I didn't have one.

I had two brothers, Vesper and Vinnie. Vesper was older than me and top dog. Cool, clever and funny, he was everything I wasn't. Then there was Vinnie, my baby brother. Vinnie was a hypochondriac – someone who thinks they're ill all the time, even when they're not – so he walked around all day, holding a tissue to his nose, terrified of catching a sniffle. I was baffled why he worried about it so much because we'd all had injections to stop us getting ill.

I had an older sister called Vicky, who was kind, patient and lovely. She hated Violet picking on me and often told her off. Finally, there was Violet, the baby and the bully of the family. Violet was blonde and pretty, and she knew it. She'd tell me how fat and stupid I was. In fact, she said it so much that I started to believe her. All our names began with a 'V' because we were the 'V' litter – the pups in each litter were all given a name using the same letter. In the 'A' litter there was Alfie, Albert, Abigail and Amy. But names beginning with a 'V' are difficult to think of. I think they ran out of boys' names when they got to me because I was called Valdez, which I hated. In fact, I hated it so much that I asked everyone to call me 'Dez' for short, and everyone did – everyone apart from Violet.

Suddenly, one of the puppy handlers zoomed into view. She was carrying something – a set of bright red feeding bowls. Breakfast had arrived! My mouth watered as I ran over eagerly towards my dish. I knew it was mine because they always put me on the end of the line to keep me away from the others' food.

'NOM, NOM, NOM...' I gulped. I didn't even pause for breath until it had gone. Licking my lips, I glanced up to see Vinnie standing there, staring forlornly at his food.

'Don't you want that?' I asked, pointing to it.

'No, I think I feel a bit... ill,' Vinnie whined. He wiped his brow dramatically with a scrunched-up tissue. 'I think I'll just go and have a lie down.'

'You can finish mine off too, if you want, Dez?' Vicky called.

Thankfully, my ears were big enough to hear even though my nose was deep in Vinnie's bowl, snuffling up his breakfast.

'Just watch out for the puppy handlers,' she whispered, looking over one shoulder. 'They like us to eat our own food, but I'm absolutely stuffed!'

So I ran over to Vicky's bowl before she could change her mind and hoovered up the lot within seconds.

'Nothing left here for you, Dez,' Vesper said, when he noticed me gazing at his bowl. 'So you can jog on,' he laughed, belching loudly.

'Violet, have you finished?'

She turned to me and narrowed her eyes. 'I'm stuffed too, but YOU'RE not having it!'

'But if you don't want it, then it'll go to waste,' I gasped because the thought of throwing away good food horrified me.

'I don't care. I'd rather the bin had it than you, you greedy lump of lard!'

'*Violet!*' The voice was so loud and unexpected it startled us all. We immediately stopped in our tracks and turned around.

It was Mum.

'If Dez is still hungry and you're not, then let him have it. And stop being so mean!'

Violet looked up at her with puppy-dog eyes and smiled sweetly.

'Yes, Mum. Sorry, Mum.' She smiled sweetly, before sticking her tongue out at me.

'NOM, NOM, NOM...'

I scoffed up the rest of her food before Violet could stop me. Breakfast done, I got down to the most important jobs of the day, playing and watching CBeebies on the telly.

'*Turn to the right and wave your hands in the air like you just don't care...*' one of the presenters sang. Dressed in a brightly coloured suit, he had mad carrot-and-green coloured hair. He looked a bit odd, like me, but I thought he was fantastic! I laughed and waggled my bum as I followed his every word.

'*Touch your toes, and then your knees. Stretch up to the stars, look and see, put your arms out and pretend you're a tree...*' he sang.

'What on earth are you doing?' Violet hissed, bumping hard against me.

'I'm being a tree.'

'Ha! You're as thick as a tree trunk! VALLLLDEZZZZ...' she crowed, stretching out my name, shouting it loud so everyone could hear.

I stopped being a tree and planted my paws back down on the ground. But Violet didn't move, instead she stood there, looking me up and down.

'Er, we're playing hide and seek, do you want to join in?' she asked suddenly.

I was flabbergasted. '*What*? You want me to join in your game?' I repeated, thinking I'd misheard her.

'Yeah, sure, why not?'

'Okay!' I replied, grateful to be asked.

I looked over her shoulder and spotted a sheet of newspaper lying on the floor in a corner of the puppy pen. Violet turned her back and began to count, so I ran over and wrapped myself up in it, like a Labrador sausage roll.

'18...19...' she continued, both paws covering her eyes. '20... Coming, ready or not!'

I put a paw over my mouth to stifle my giggles as she approached. Vicky was hiding under a cream blanket but you could see the square shape of her Labrador head a mile away. Vinnie refused to play because he said he felt sick and took to his bed, but Vesper squeezed in around the back of it. He'd asked Mum and Vinnie to camouflage him, covering his head and body with teddies.

'Now, let me see, where would they hide...?' Violet asked, strolling over towards me.

Dying to laugh, I clasped a paw against my mouth. I held my breath because I didn't want the paper to crinkle around my belly and give my secret hiding place away.

'Hmmm, I think I need to sit down and have a think about this one,' she said, parking her big bum on top of the paper and me. But she was heavier than I'd thought, and soon her weight was crushing my ribs. I wanted to shout out and tell her to get off, but I couldn't. Instead, I held my breath but soon my face had turned bright purple, trying to hold it in. Seconds later, it came rushing out, leaving me flat, like a deflated Labrador balloon!

'Okay, you've found me,' I said, waiting for her to stand up and get off, only she didn't. Instead, she pressed down even harder, flattening me like a squished hot dog.

'Violet, I'm underneath you. You're hurting me!' I cried, but she wasn't listening.

In the end, Mum came over, picked her up by the scruff of the neck and pulled her off me. I'm certain Violet knew I was there; she was just being horrible.

The following day, I tried to avoid her, but she followed me around like a shadow. In a bid to get away, I stuck my head out in between the bars at the front of the puppy pen. I was still looking up, watching CBeebies on the TV, when a voice called out.

'Hi, I'm Star, what's your name?' it said.

My head was between the bars but I twisted it slightly and that's when I saw her – a beautiful golden Labrador

7

pup, staring straight back at me with honey-brown coloured eyes.

'Wow, you're beautiful!' I blurted out, without even thinking.

It was true; Star was the prettiest pup I'd ever seen.

'And so are you,' she replied kindly.

I shook my head but my big ears got in the way and slapped me hard around the face. 'No, I'm not. All my brothers and sisters are beautiful, fluffy and golden like you, but I'm ugly, with stupid, big ears,' I said, shaking them to show her.

'No, you're not, you're amazing! You look really cool. I'm just a boring sandy colour, I'd love to look like you. It's weird because even though I'm golden, all my sisters and brothers are black Labradors, like you. I'd love to be like you because then I'd fit in, so you see, I'm just like you because I'm the odd one out too!'

I shook my head in disbelief. 'Maybe we should swap places?'

'Yeah, maybe,' Star chuckled.

'I'm Dez, by the way,' I said, sticking my paw out for her to shake, only it wouldn't stretch far enough so I put it back down on the ground again. 'Well,' I explained, 'my real name is Valdez, but I don't like it very much, so I prefer to be called Dez.'

'So, you're one of the "V" pups who live next-door?'

'Yep.' I nodded. 'There's me, Vinnie, Vesper, Vicky and Violet,' I said, counting them off one by one against each claw.

Star's face clouded over.

'Not Violent! Erm, I mean Violet.'

She gasped, her eyes wide with horror.

'Yeah, she's my little sister. Why, have you heard of her?'

'Who hasn't? Everyone knows who she is, because she's the biggest bully in here!'

That made me laugh. 'Yeah, you're right there. She's horrible to everyone but she particularly hates me. She calls me fat and says my ears stick out, just like a bat!'

Star shook her head. 'That's horrible! Listen, there's nothing wrong with you or your, erm, ears,' she said, noticing them for the first time. 'It's your sister who's ugly. She's ugly on the inside *and* the outside – all bullies are.'

I nodded. 'You're right there, the only person Violet loves is herself.'

'So, are you excited about becoming a guide dog?' she asked, changing the subject.

I nodded my head. 'Yes, it's all I've ever wanted to be. It's what we were born to do, isn't it? If I couldn't become one of them, then I don't know what I'd do. But I worry about it all the time.'

'Why?'

'Because, what if I don't make the grade? What if I fail my exams, what then? No one would want me then.' My stomach tightened with anxiety as I spoke.

'Don't be daft.' Star laughed. 'Of course someone would want you. You're funny, you're cute, you've got silly ears which flap around...'

I smiled – she wasn't being unkind, she was just trying to make me laugh.

'But what if I don't pass, Star? What will become of me?'

'But you will pass, because you're clever. Anyone can see that.'

Just then, one of the puppy handlers wandered over towards both pens. Dinner was served.

'Now then, Dezzy boy, are you ready for some food, hmmm?' the worker said, giving me a gentle pat on the top of my head.

So I wagged my tail to show I was. I loved dinner and breakfast. In fact, I loved *all* food.

'Well, just you pull your head out of the bars then, so I can get in,' she said.

Like a small car in reverse, I backed my body up, but as I tried to pull out my head, I realised it was stuck. With all my might, I pulled again, but the bars pushed hard against my ginormous ears, trapping them. No matter how hard I tried, my huge, square-shaped head wouldn't budge.

'Oh no, you're not stuck, are you?' the lady gasped.

I nodded glumly because I felt pretty stupid, especially in front of Star, who'd just been telling me how clever I was. Then I watched as the lady placed both bowls of food on the floor, but far enough out of reach to stop me from snaffling them. She called out to a man who came over to help. He held my head while she wrapped both hands around my belly and tried her hardest to yank me out. They pushed and pulled for ages, but it was no good – I was stuck!

'I think someone's been eating too many dinners,' the woman chuckled, as the man disappeared off to fetch a sponge, some water and soap.

'Oh no, I'm going to be stuck here forever!' I wailed as Violet began to laugh behind me.

'Look at old fat bum,' she crowed.

I pulled again, but it was no good. My big ears were firmly wedged between the metal bars. Now I was well and truly stuck.

It took a whole bar of soap, a lot of bubbles and a bit of brute force. My head was soaked in slippy white foam, but somehow they managed to pull me free. My ears were full of bubbles, but other than that, I was as good as new and cleaner than I'd been in ages.

'I think someone needs to go on a diet,' Violet sneered later, as I snuggled down next to Mum for a cuddle. She waited until Mum wasn't looking and poked me hard in the ribs with a sharpened claw. It made my belly wobble like a jelly.

'You're useless,' she whispered, so the others wouldn't hear. 'Anyway, I've told you, you'll never become a guide dog because you're fat and stupid. It's the big test next week and you're bound to fail. If you fail then they'll send you away from here, forever! You'll never see us or Mum again...'

But I'd stopped listening.

'Hang on, what test?' I said, sitting up.

'Puppy SATS! Why, haven't you been practising? I've been practising for weeks and I know it all off by heart,' she crowed.

I gulped because I didn't know what she was talking about. No one had said anything to me about a puppy test.

'Violet,' I said, beginning to panic, 'will you help me practise? Will you show me what to do?'

'No chance! I'm not helping you because if you fail then they'll send you away and I won't ever have to see your ugly mug ever again.'

With that, she turned and fell asleep.

But I couldn't sleep because I was worried – worried about Puppy SATS.

What if I failed? Then I'd never become a guide dog. What would I do then? Who would have me? I'd be sent away and I'd never see Mum or my brothers and sisters again.

While the others slept soundly with their heads against Mum's warm body, I was so worried that it made my stomach hurt. I was exhausted but eventually I fell into a fitful night's sleep. But then I had nightmares. I heard Violet laughing as I was picked up and carted off in a van. I was so scared and tired in the morning that by the time breakfast had arrived, I'd completely lost my appetite.

'What's the matter, Dezzy boy, not eating? That's not like you,' the handler said.

I turned and walked away from my bowl. As I wandered over towards my bed and flopped inside, my mind whirred with worry. The others seemed confused as they finished their breakfasts, but I didn't want to talk to them because I was all churned up inside. I couldn't face them or food because I felt as sick as a dog – sick with nerves. If I failed the test then I'd never become a guide dog and my dream would be over before it had even begun.

CHAPTER 2

PUPPY SATS

With the test looming over me, I tried my best to remember what it took to be a good guide dog.

Number 1. *Looking all around.* I scribbled at the top of the list.

Number 2. *Listening.*

Number 3. *Being a good friend*, I wrote, but then I stopped because I couldn't think of a number four.

I held the pencil in my paw and scratched the back of my ear with the tip of it.

'Whatcha doing, Dez?' a voice called from over my shoulder.

It was Vicky.

'Nothing much, I'm just trying to remember what it takes to be a good guide dog.'

I sharpened up the end of my pencil. Wooden shavings curled out in small ribbons and fell against the piece of paper in my hand. I took a deep breath and blew them away.

'What for?' she asked, with a puzzled look on her face.

'Because we've got some exams coming up, Violet said so.'

Vicky shook her head. 'Oh, Dez, you're such a worrier! Anyway, it's not a written test, it's a physical one.'

'Physical?'

'Yeah, it's to test how good you are at running through tunnels, whether you know your name, that sort of thing.'

I placed the pencil down on the floor.

'So we won't have to write anything?' I gasped, sitting up with my back against the side of the pen.

'No, not at all! Just be yourself and you'll be fine.'

'But... but... Violet said...'

Vicky waved her paw as if trying to swat Violet's name away.

'Oh, don't listen to a word she says, because you know what she's like. Violet says things to wind you up, because she knows how much you worry.'

I scratched my head.

'So, I don't have to do this sort of thing?' I asked, pointing towards the list.

'Nope.'

'So, would you help me?' I begged. 'I mean, would you help me pass the exam?'

Vicky wrapped a comforting paw around my shoulder. 'Of course I will, little bruv. Now, stop worrying and you'll be fine.'

For the rest of the day, Vicky had me running through tunnels we'd built using bits of cardboard. My stomach got wedged in the middle of them a few times, but by now, I was determined to become the best guide dog ever! I even started to watch how much I ate. And I practised until I became as fast as I could. In fact, I was so fast, I was knocking things over.

'No, Dez, you need to slow down if you want to do well,' Mum called from her bed.

But Violet disagreed. 'No, you need to go faster. In fact, the faster, the better! The quicker you are, the better guide dog you'll make.'

'Really?' I asked, a little surprised, 'it's just that Mum said—'

'Oh, ignore Mum! She doesn't know what she's talking about. Besides, she doesn't have to do these tests, *we* do. No, the faster you go, the better.'

Violet's words stayed in my head as I thanked her for her help. On the day of the test, I was raring to go and wound up as tight as a top on a bottle of fizzy pop. I watched from the side, running everything through in my head. Vesper went first but he didn't seem very fast. He wasn't as fast as me, but I knew from the look on the puppy handler's face that he'd done well.

'Good boy, Vesper,' she said, giving him a pat on the top of his head.

He wagged his tail in delight.

'Now then,' she said, looking down at the clipboard she held. 'Valdez, which one of you is Valdez?'

I gulped and stepped forward. Now it was my turn to shine. As I waddled over, I heard someone snigger; I turned to see Violet holding a paw over her mouth but as soon as our eyes met, she withdrew it and gave me a quick thumbs-up. It gave me extra courage to carry on.

'Right, Valdez, I need you to go through this tunnel,' the lady said, peering through it, tapping her hand against the ground at the other end.

I wanted to smile and wave at her, but I knew I had to concentrate. So I took a deep breath and with all my might, went running straight into the plastic tube. I was bounding along so fast that my back legs couldn't keep up, and soon I'd tumbled over, landing flat on my back. The tunnel began to turn like a washing machine on full spin. It rolled out of control until I was falling over in the middle of it. My ears got tangled up beneath my head and I started to feel sick and dizzy. The examiner must have grabbed hold of it to stop it from spinning because suddenly it came to an abrupt halt. I clambered up onto four paws. Still feeling a little dizzy, I staggered out. Although my paws were on solid ground, the world was still spinning as I tried to focus on the examiner.

'Er, right,' she said, the disappointment obvious in her voice. Then I heard a snort of laughter and turned to see Violet clutching her sides. I shot her a stern look.

'You need to go faster,' she hissed, with a paw against the side of her mouth so the others wouldn't hear.

I knew she was right; I'd been too slow, and that's why I'd made such a mess of it.

The next part of the test was recall, or answering to my name. I was determined to do well, but as soon as the puppy handler called out Valdez, I was so busy thinking about what I needed to do that I forgot it was my actual name.

'VALDEZ!' the woman repeated.

I looked over my shoulder, wondering if she was talking to someone else, but I was puzzled when I saw there was no one there, only me. That's when I realised, she *was* talking to me, Dez... Valdez!

'Coming!' I woofed.

I ran over to her as fast as my legs would carry me. With no obstacles to trip me up, I'd reached her within seconds. But running was easy, it was the stopping I wasn't so good at. Instead, when I tried to put the brakes on, I ran past her in a doggy blur and crashed straight into the opposite wall, headbutting it hard. I shook my ears as my head rang inside, like a bell. Soon, all I could see were white stars, only not of the puppy variety, but actual real-life sparkling stars, dancing around in front of my eyes.

'Right, okay. You're certainly an eager little chap, who's willing to please,' the woman said, ticking something off her list.

I thought she must be paying me a compliment, but when I noticed the look on her face, I realised I'd messed up again. It took me a few moments to come around. I shook my head but my elephant ears slapped me hard around the face, making me feel even more stupid.

'Valdez,' the trainer said, trying to snap me out of my daze, 'I need you to watch this.' She pulled something out of her pocket. It was a round object attached to a piece of string, which she began to swing in front of my eyes. I watched as it swung from side to side.

Don't take your eyes off it, I told myself. *Don't take your eyes off it, not even for a second.*

'Good! Clever boy!' the woman encouraged.

I stared even harder until my eyes began to ache. But the more I stared, the more tired I felt. I yawned, then, without warning, the room blurred.

I don't know how long I was asleep, but a sharp pain in one of my ears woke me: it was Violet nipping me.

'Where am I?' I asked, rubbing my eyes.

'You're in the puppy pen. Someone had to pick you up and carry you back to bed.'

'Eh?'

'You fell asleep, stupid! You failed the test because you fell asleep, right in the middle of the floor.'

'I didn't!' I gasped. Suddenly I remembered the swinging circle and my eyelids growing heavy. 'What did the woman say? I mean, how did I do in the test?'

But Violet simply threw back her head and snorted with laughter. 'You failed, Valdez. What did you expect? You were fast asleep, snoring, in the middle of the test. You'll never be a guide dog now, unlike me,' she added, polishing her claws against the fur on her chest. 'You see, *I* passed with flying colours.'

At this I panicked because becoming a guide dog was all I'd ever wanted. I was rubbish at everything else, apart from eating.

'But what does it mean?' I cried.

'It means,' Violet smirked, covering my eyes with my enormous ears, 'that you'll *never* become a guide dog. That's it, you've blown your chance. Your dream is over!'

After she'd left, I buried my face between my paws and began to cry. I cried because I'd messed up and now there was no going back. The others were watching the puppy tests, so I was all alone... or so I thought.

'Hey, Dez, is that you?' called a voice.

It was Star.

I wiped my eyes, took a deep breath and poked my head out of the front of the bars to see her.

'Why are you crying?'

'I wasn't,' I sniffed. 'I've just got a bit of a cold.'

Star shook her head. 'Dez, I heard you. Listen, don't cry, because everything will be alright, I promise.'

'But the puppy test – I failed,' I told her, my voice quivering, and with tears in my eyes. 'I'll never be a guide dog now,' I sniffed.

'Of course you will! They knew you were nervous, lots of pups are, so they're going to give you a second chance.'

'But how do you know?'

Star put a paw up against the side of her mouth and whispered: 'Because I saw the re-test list and your name is on it.'

'WHAAT?' I gasped.

'SHUSSHHH!' she hissed. 'Don't tell anyone, because I'll get in trouble. There was a list of names, and yours was right at the top.'

'Yes!' I grinned, punching the air. 'So they're going to give me another chance? I can still be a guide dog?'

'Yes,' said Star, 'so stop worrying, and start practising! You can do this, Dez. You can become the best guide dog this place has ever seen.'

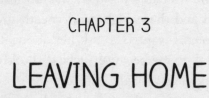

CHAPTER 3

LEAVING HOME

S tar was right, because only a few days later the examiner
let me try again. The second time, I slowed down
because Vicky had told me to.

'But, Violet—' I argued.

'Don't believe a word she says,' Vicky warned. 'She's out
to try and ruin things for you. Just do as I say, be yourself
and you'll be fine.'

And I was. At one point when I was heading into the
tunnel I tripped up, but as I stumbled, I remembered what
Vicky had said, stopped and took a deep breath. Then I
set off again, only this time a little slower. Thankfully, the
rest of the exam went fine and I passed. I even remembered
to answer to my posh boy's name – Valdez. I didn't care
what the examiner called me, so long as I didn't put a
paw wrong.

When I'd finished, I got a well-earned pat on the head.

As I turned my face, I noticed something written on a piece of paper in the woman's hand. It was the list of puppies to be re-tested and there, right underneath my name, was another – Violet. I wanted to ask her about it, but Violet refused to speak to me because Vicky had told her off over the nasty tricks she'd played.

'I didn't mean to get her into trouble, Vicky,' I sighed. 'I'm sure she was just trying to help.'

'No, Dez,' Vicky insisted. 'Violet knew exactly what she was doing. There's only one dog Violet is interested in and that's herself. Besides,' she added, pulling something out from behind her back. 'Look what I found hidden in her bed.'

'Mr Roo Roo, erm, I mean Rupert!' I gasped.

It was my special teddy. I'd had him since I was born but I thought I'd lost him. I ran over, grabbed him from Vicky's paws and gave him an extra-big cuddle.

'But what was Mr Roo... I mean, Rupert, what was he doing in Violet's bed?'

Vicky sighed. 'That's what I've been trying to tell you. Violet realised just how much you loved Rupert so she hid him from you. That's what she's like, Dez, can't you see? She's horrible!'

'But I don't understand. Why would she do that to me?'

'Look, Violet wanted you to fail, but you haven't, have you? That's because you're special, just like Mum said. You watch, one day you'll outshine us all.'

'Do you really think so?' I asked, Rupert dangling by one arm from my mouth.

'Yes, I do. Now, stop worrying about Violet because she's not worth it. Instead, think about what you need to pack because we'll be leaving in a few days.'

My stomach somersaulted with nerves. I'd completely forgotten – it was almost time to leave my puppy family and go to my new home with my new family. They'd be my puppy walkers for the next year. That night, once the others had fallen asleep, I pulled out Rupert and cuddled him. I thought no one had seen me, only I was wrong.

'You found Mr Roo Roo?' Mum whispered, looking down at me. 'I thought you'd lost him. Where was he?'

But I didn't want to get Violet into trouble, so I told a fib.

'Vicky found him,' I explained. Then I changed the subject because I didn't want her to ask me any more difficult questions. 'Do you think they'll be nice, my puppy-walking family?'

'Of course.' Mum smiled. 'They'll be lovely! The people at Guide Dogs pick out families who love animals.'

She stooped down to give me a kiss. Her long, gravelly tongue felt warm and comforting against the soft, puppy fur on top of my head.

'Now go to sleep,' she said, nuzzling the side of her nose against my face.

I shut my eyes, but try as I might, I couldn't sleep because I just couldn't imagine life without my puppy family. The following day, I was still anxious as I packed my suitcase for the trip.

'Do you think my new mum will love me as much as you do?'

'Yes, because puppy walkers love all dogs, especially cute little ones like you.'

'Even pups with big ears?' I smirked, giving them a shake.

Mum laughed. 'Especially pups with big ears! They love them the most.'

'But I'll miss it here. I'll miss you, and Star – I'll miss you all.' My voice tailed off as an awful thought popped into my head. 'What if I don't like it? What if I don't fit in there?'

'Dez, have you packed Mr Roo Roo?' Mum asked, interrupting me.

'Shush!' I whispered, putting a paw to my mouth. I looked over my shoulder to check no one had heard.

'Oh, Dez!' sighed Mum. 'It's okay to have a favourite teddy. All children have them, it's nothing to be ashamed of.'

'I know, I'll take him. Just don't tell the others, please!' I begged.

I could just imagine what Violet would say if she knew.

'Okay, and what about your favourite blankie?'

I felt the blood drain from my face.

'What?'

'Your special blankie, your own special snuggles.'

'Mum!' I sighed, rolling my eyes because she was talking to me like I was still a baby, 'I'm a big dog now, I'll be fine without it.'

'Okay, but you better take it, in case of emergencies – in case you feel a little homesick.'

But I shook my head. 'No, I'll be fine. Besides, I've got to be brave and strong if I want to become a guide dog. I bet guide dogs don't have teddies and blankets.'

'I bet they do.' Mum smirked. 'Here,' she said, passing me the knitted blanket. 'Just pop it in there,' she added, her paw pointing towards a gap at the side of the case. 'It won't take up too much space.'

'Okay,' I whispered. 'But promise me you won't tell the others.'

'I won't,' Mum whispered, holding up a paw, 'guide dog promise.'

My suitcase was quite full, but it had everything I needed, including a photo of Mum and Dad. My father was already a fully qualified guide dog, but he lived and worked away with his owner so I'd never met him. But Mum had sent him photos of us all.

'You will tell Dad that I passed my test, won't you?'

Mum nodded.

'And you'll text me, promise?'

'I promise. Now, are you sure you've packed everything?' she said, checking my case over one last time. 'Here,' she whispered. I watched as she dug her paw beneath her back legs and rooted around for something underneath her blanket. Moments later, she'd pulled out a packet of dog treats. 'Here's a little something for you, but don't tell the others, and don't eat them all at once because they'll make you sick.'

As I took the packet from her paw, I nuzzled into her side. I gave her a cuddle, although inside I felt scared and teary. Now my case was packed, it meant I was even closer to leaving home. I was frightened because I didn't know when I'd see my lovely mum again.

How would I cope?

'I love you, Dez,' she said, wrapping her front paws around my shoulders.

I nuzzled into her and smelt her lovely thick, warm fur. It stuck out and tickled my nose and I felt the urge to sneeze, but I didn't want Mum to let go, not ever, because I felt safe.

'You're my special boy,' she whispered. 'Just be yourself, Dez, and everyone will love you.'

I sighed happily, wrapped in Mum's embrace, but then

she pulled away and gripped the top of my front legs with her paws.

'And whatever you do, promise me you'll stop worrying?'

'Okay, I'll try.'

Mum licked the side of my head.

'Now try and get some sleep because it's a big day tomorrow.'

Before I went to bed, I popped my head out of the front of the puppy pen and called Star's name.

'I guess this is goodbye then,' I mumbled sadly.

Her head bobbed out to face me.

'Why, do you leave tomorrow?'

'Yep.'

'And how do you feel about it?'

I shrugged my shoulders. 'Dunno, I'm a bit scared, I suppose,' I said, gazing glumly at the ground.

'But your puppy walkers, you've met them already, haven't you?'

I nodded my head. Niki, her husband Jon and their three children had already been in to say 'hello'.

'Yes, they seem really, really nice.'

'So, what are you worried about then? You'll be fine. Besides, it's only a year before you'll be back in training and I bet it passes like that,' she said with a click of her claws.

'Do you really think so?'

'I know so, Dez. And don't forget, I'll be here waiting for you when you get back because I'm going to be a brilliant guide dog, just like you.'

'Yeah,' I said, brightening up a little. 'So this isn't really goodbye then, is it?'

Star shook her head. 'No, not at all! Listen, I'd wish you luck, but you won't need it because you're going to be brilliant.'

'Thanks, Star, and I promise I'll text you when I get there.'

'You better, Dezzy boy, otherwise I'll come looking for you!' she cried, pretending to growl.

'Night, night, then.' I yawned.

I lifted up my paw and we inched up to the side of our pens, enough that our paw pads were touching.

'I'm gonna miss you,' I said, the words choking in my throat.

'Me too. But Dez...' she murmured.

'What?'

'Thank you for being my best friend.'

I grinned as a nice, warm, fuzzy feeling melted inside my stomach.

'No, thank *you*, Star! You're right, you know. This isn't goodbye, it's just so long for now.'

The following morning, my sisters and brothers lined up, as one by one, we all took it in turns to say farewell to Mum. I tried to be brave but I'd already started to sob before I reached the front of the line. Mum hugged me so tight that I thought she'd never let go – and I didn't want her to. After I'd dried my tears, it was time to say goodbye to each other.

'Take care, mate,' said Vesper, picking up his suitcase, fist bumping my paw as he passed.

'You too, Vesp! And I'll see you soon, when we come back for guide-dog training,' I called.

Vesper smiled and nodded back at me.

'You betcha!'

'Take it easy, Vinnie,' I said, stepping forward to try and hug him.

'I don't feel very well,' Vinnie complained, backing away from me warily. He held a tissue to his nose and gave it an enormous snotty blow.

'You'll be fine,' I said, trying to reassure him.

'But I feel sick already, and I haven't even got in the car yet!' He panicked and turned towards Mum. 'Did you pack my travel sickness tablets?'

'*Yes*, Vinnie!' Mum snapped, a little impatient. 'Now, hurry up. Go and join Vesper because you don't want to be late, do you?'

Vinnie nodded as I went back in for a big hug.

'No, no, don't get too close! I don't want to catch any of your bugs. By the way, you are up to date with your inoculations, aren't you?'

'Yes, Vinnie,' I grinned, grabbing hold of his shoulders before he could object.

'Ooh, not too hard! Please don't hug me too hard because it hurts. I think I've bruised a rib or something.'

I tried not to laugh because he never changed. Vinnie was a moaner, but I knew I'd miss him. Moments later, another figure appeared – it was Vicky.

'Oh, Dez, what am I going to do without you?' she said, beginning to sob. 'I'll miss you *so* much!'

'Hey, don't worry about me, just take care of yourself, that's what you told me! Remember?'

Vicky stepped forward and hugged me so hard, I thought she'd break my ribs.

'Ooh, not too tight!' I gasped.

Vicky wiped her tears and began to giggle.

'*Don't*,' she sniggered, 'you sound just like Vinnie!'

'I know, but that's quite a strong hug you've got there.'

We both stood for a moment, neither of us knowing what to say. Out of all my family, besides Mum, I knew I'd miss Vicky the most. Finally, after what seemed ages, my voice broke the silence.

'Thanks, Vicky.'

She looked puzzled. 'What for?'

'Thanks for everything. You know, helping me pass the test and everything.'

But Vicky waved her paw in the air as though it were nothing.

'Don't be daft, you passed it yourself, Dez. You just needed to believe in yourself, that's all.'

I looked at the ground, because we both knew it was untrue. Without Vicky, there was no way I would have got through it.

'I'm so lucky to have a big sister like you.'

'Nonsense!' she said, giving me a playful push. 'Now promise me you'll text and let me know you got there okay? You've got my mobile number, haven't you?'

At this I nodded. I was just about to reply when Violet zoomed into view.

'What mobile number? I haven't got your number,' she said, both paws resting on her hips. She turned to Vicky, waiting for an answer.

'That,' said Vicky, poking Violet hard in the chest, 'is because I. Don't. Want. You. To. Have. It.' She said each word with a prod of her paws.

'Why, are you frightened I'll do better than you, or summat?' Violet sneered.

I stood in the middle, not knowing quite what to do. Of course I hated seeing my sisters argue, but once they'd started I knew there was no stopping them.

'And I found Dez's teddy hidden in your bed! Why did you steal it?' Vicky argued back.

'Because teddies are for babies and he isn't a baby anymore.' Violet sniffed, looking back at me. 'He's supposed to be a guide dog, but that's a joke because he's nothing but a big, fat embarrassment.'

'*Violet!*'

Mum's voice came out really loud and it startled us all. It also stopped the argument stone-dead. She turned to Violet and ordered her to pick up her bag and leave.

'I sincerely hope that they teach you some manners at your new home, young lady!' she scolded.

Violet pulled a face, picked up her bag and stormed off towards the door.

'Laterzzzzz, losers!' she said, holding up a paw without turning around.

I watched as she marched out of the puppy centre, angrily slinging a bright pink, sparkly handbag across one shoulder.

'Come on then, you two,' said Mum, looking down at Vicky and me. 'You better hurry up, because your families will be waiting for you. Now, get yourselves off! I know you'll both do me proud,' she blubbed. Mum was trying her best to hold back her tears but I knew she was upset. She turned, walked away, and slumped down heavily in her bed. It broke my heart to see her there staring sadly into thin air – all of her children gone.

'Bye, Mum, I love you!' I called, as we headed for the door.

As we'd reached it, I turned towards Vicky for the last time.

'Right, well, I suppose this is it, then?' I said, wishing the sad feeling would go away.

'Take care, my special bruv. Love you loads!' cried Vicky, emotion choking her voice.

Thankfully, my puppy walkers arrived to collect me first, which meant I didn't have to be the last one standing there, waving everyone off.

'Hello, Dez,' a lovely kind woman said, kneeling down to pat me on the top of my head. I recognised her immediately – it was Niki, my new puppy-walker mum.

'She looks brilliant,' Vicky whispered, giving me the thumbs-up behind Niki's back.

'She *is*!' I grinned, before climbing into the back of Niki's car. 'See you all in a year!' I yelled, as I waved madly from the back window.

Everyone waved back, apart from Violet, who stood there scowling.

The car fired into life and slowly wound its way along the tarmac drive, away from the puppy centre and towards my new home and new life. When we were finally out of view, I sat down on the back seat, undid the latch on my suitcase and took out my teddy and blankie.

Mum had been right, I was glad I had them both with me!

CHAPTER 4

SCARY SUPERMARKETS

I arrived at my new home in March. It was cold, so Niki wrapped me up in my favourite blanket and carried me into the house. She put me down on the floor, but there was so much to see that I ran from room to room. There were a few things I recognised from the guide-dog puppy centre, including the washing machine and TV.

I wonder if they watch CBeebies?

Although I was nervous because it was all new to me, Niki gave me plenty of cuddles, which made me feel loads better. As an added bonus she'd also bought me lots of new toys to play with.

'Now, Dez,' she explained, 'the children will be home soon, so you'll get lots more cuddles.'

She was right. As soon as Molly, Harry and Sam burst in through the door, I was smothered with love.

'Oh, he's gorgeous, isn't he?' Molly gasped, kissing the top of my head. Molly was the youngest, aged ten years old. Then there was Harry, twelve, and fourteen-year-old Sam.

I wondered if anyone would say anything about my stupid big ears, but no one did, because my puppy walkers loved me for who I was.

Jon came home from work and soon we were just like a regular family, but I was so exhausted from the long journey and all the extra attention that I curled up in my new big bed and fell fast asleep. The following morning, I woke up and texted Vicky. The pads of my paws typed each letter quickly.

Hi, V, Love it here. Itz brill. I get tonz of food, cuddles, & kisses. I've got my own bed. Itz great! Hope u like yours 2. Txt me soon. Miss u! Dez xxx

I buried my mobile under my blanket, but moments later it buzzed with Vicky's reply.

Hi little bruv, great 2 hear from u. It's great here 2. I'm getting loads of cuddles & the food's really good. Can't wait to c u again soon! Love your big sis xxx

I was so happy to hear from Vicky that, as soon as I'd read her message I sent another message, this time to Star.

Hi Star, guess who? Itz Dezzy boy. I'm in my new ome. Oops... I mean home with an h! Howz puppy school? Do u miss me? I miss u! Love your best pal xxx

Once I'd pressed send, I texted Mum.

Hello Mum, itz Dez. I'm in my new home and my new puppy walker mum is lovely, just like you! Don't worry, she looks after me really well and gives me lots of nice things to eat. I've eaten my bag of treats already. Sorry, but they were lovely. U were right about Mr Roo Roo and blankie, I'm glad I have them. Miss u loads but I'll see you soon when I come back to be a guide dog, just like Dad. Dez xxx

Just as I'd finished, Star replied. The phone buzzed in my paw as I opened up the message.

Hi Dez! I'm so glad to hear from u. I miss u like mad! It's boring here without u. What's it like to be a big, grown-up, eh? Is it good? I leave here in a few days and I can't wait! See u when we both go to big school. Star xx P.s: Did u hear about Violent? I mean Violet?

I didn't know what she was talking about, so I texted her straight back.

No, what about Violet? Whatz happened?

My mobile buzzed.

She's not going to be a guide dog after all. She failed...

'What!' I gasped, my eyes wide with shock.

...It's true, Dez, the text continued. *Everyone's talking about it. I'm not sure what happened but she never passed her puppy SATS after all. Anyway, if you hear anything, let me know, and remember, it's not goodbye, just so long for now, love your best friend forever, S xxx*

Although I'd just texted Mum, I sent her another asking about Violet, and I didn't have long to wait for a reply.

Hello, my lovely boy. I hope they're looking after you and that you're eating properly (but not too much!)... lol! Yes, it's true about Violet. She knew she'd already failed when you left, but she didn't want anyone to know. That's why she was mean to you and your sister. But all is not lost, because Violet's going to become a buddy dog. She'll be a friend to those who'll need it most. She texted me last night, and I think she realises how mean she was. Honestly, Dez, I think she's changed. If you want, I can text you her mobile number. Look after yourself & call me if you need anything. Love you to the moon and back, Mum xxx

I asked Mum for Violet's number but I wasn't sure what I should say, so I decided to think about it for a bit. The next week was a blur of activity. With the children busy at school, my new mum took me out shopping to the supermarket. Unlike other dogs, guide dog pups wear a distinctive blue jacket with the words '*Guide Dog in Training*' written on the side – it made me feel very important. I realised it was like wearing my very own special VIP doggy pass. Everywhere we went, people would stop Niki to ask about me.

'I'm his puppy walker,' she explained. 'I look after him for the first year.'

Soon, I'd started to love all the attention, especially when Niki carried me in her arms.

'Oh, isn't he cute?' the children would say, begging to have a stroke.

It's funny, because I'd never thought as myself as cute, but people, especially children, seemed to think that I was. One day, a few weeks after I'd arrived at my new home, Niki decided to take me to the supermarket again, only this time, she didn't carry me.

'You're getting a bit heavy now, Dez,' she decided, putting me on the floor. 'Besides, you need to learn how to walk around a supermarket.'

I puffed out my chest and held my head high. Even though I was only as tall as the first shelf on one of the supermarket aisles, I felt very important in my blue jacket and with my special guide-dog lead. I was determined to make Niki proud and try my very best. The floor felt cold and slippy beneath my paws, and as soon as I began to walk, my four legs started sliding in different directions.

'Whoa!' I cried, as my paws scrambled against the slippy surface. Soon, I'd landed flat on my bum. I felt like a right banana!

'Oh Dez, are you okay?' asked Niki, scooping me back up. She planted me back on all fours, but my legs felt a little unsteady.

THUD! I landed hard against the floor with a clatter.

Eventually I worked out if I put my paws down hard and flat then they wouldn't slide out to the sides.

'That's better, well done!' Niki encouraged.

I was just getting the hang of it when I heard a terrible noise. It began as a low rumble but soon all I could hear was a loud, terrifying screech as metal scraped against the supermarket floor. I looked up and saw what I thought was a large iron horse heading straight towards me.

'Niki! Niki!' I whimpered as it grew closer.

It looked vicious, with sharp metal bars and wheels instead of legs: a monster was chasing me! I was so frightened that I ran behind Niki, where my legs rattled like jellybeans in a glass jar. Suddenly, I felt something warm and damp. I looked down and my heart sank when I realised that I'd wet myself and now I was standing in the middle of a big yellow puddle on the supermarket floor.

'Oh, Dez!' Niki sighed. She picked me up and wiped me

down with baby wipes. Even though I was safe in her arms, I could still see the monster heading over to us. I panicked and looked from Niki to the monster and back again.

'Dez, whatever's the matter?' she asked, as I squirmed in her arms.

I couldn't take my eyes off the metal beast as it edged closer. Niki followed my gaze and realised why I was so frightened.

'Oh, Dez!' she giggled. 'Is *that* what it is? Don't be scared, it's only a shopping trolley. People use them to put food in!'

After she'd cleaned up my, er, little accident, Niki took me outside to look at the trolleys and meet the man who collected them from the car park.

'Look,' she said, pushing one with her hand. It made me

flinch but then she explained. 'It won't hurt you, it's just like a big shopping basket on wheels.'

The more I watched, the more I realised she was right. I felt a little bit silly, but to a pup my size, the trolley looked like a house on wheels.

Still, we continued to travel in the car to the supermarket so I could get used to the noise. The woman's voice shouting over the shop's loudspeakers startled me a bit to begin with, as did all the crashing and banging as humans threw tins and bottles into baskets and trolleys, but after a while I got used to it, until soon I was able to walk around confidently and help Niki with her weekly shop.

I really wanted to meet other dogs and go running in the park, but she explained I had to wait until I'd had all my jabs. It seemed to take ages, but eventually I was ready for my first trip to the park with Niki, her friend Lisa and her dog, Stan. Stan was a collie-cross and a rescue dog, which meant his original owners had decided they didn't want him. Thankfully, he was rescued by a lovely family and although his life was great again, he'd had a very different start from me.

'I don't want to talk about it, son,' he explained. 'All I would say is that it wasn't very nice, but then I met my new family. They took me in and gave me a loving home, and since then, life's never been better!' He sighed, his eyes misting over with happiness.

I felt lucky that I'd not had to go through the same thing as Stan. It made me realise just how lucky I was: not only did I have a lovely mum and puppy-walking family to look after me, I also had a great future as a guide dog, helping

someone else to lead a better life. It made me all the more
determined to pass my exams.

Stan was older than me, around four years old, so what
he'd not seen or done wasn't worth knowing about.

'What's it like down the park, Stan?' I asked, my voice
full of excitement. 'Are there swings and slides? Are there
children, grass, and...'

Stan put his paw up to stop me mid-sentence.

'All in good time! You'll soon see for yourself, but parks
are magical places where dogs like you and me are able
to run free and feel the wind in our... erm... ears,' he said,
looking over at me. 'Blimey, haven't you got big ears for
a pup?'

'Yeah, I know. You don't think the other dogs will laugh
at me, do you?'

'What? Nonsense! We get all sorts down the park – fat
dogs, thin dogs, long-haired, short-haired, and then there's
ones with fleas, and ones without. We have new breeds
of dogs whose names I can't even pronounce. You know,
posh, stuck-up dogs. There's even a few who wear clothes,
just like humans.'

'No!' I gasped.

'Seriously, just you wait and see. It's as though their fur
isn't good enough. Personally, I think they look a bit daft,
but it's their owners, you see, they like dressing them up,
even if the dogs hate it. I guess I'm a little bit old-fashioned
like that. I can't keep up with all these new-fangled trends for
fancy collars and "bling" overcoats, it's stuff and nonsense,'
he concluded. 'Anyway, you'll soon see for yourself.'

If I thought Stan had been exaggerating then I realised I was wrong when Niki pushed open the gate to the park. The place was absolutely massive, with loads of space to run around. I watched as Lisa unclipped Stan, all the while hoping that Niki would let me go for a run too.

'Go on, Dez! Just a quick one, until you get used to it,' she said, unclipping my lead.

'Thanks, Niki!'

Barking, I ran as fast as I could. I ran with Stan until I felt dizzy. As I sat down on the grass, panting, trying to catch my breath, I spotted a tiny dog walking towards us.

'Hello!' I called. 'My name's Dez. I'm new to this park, but I live around here with my puppy walkers, so I'd like to make lots of new friends. What's your name?'

But the little dog simply stared at me blankly, stuck her pointed little nose in the air, and strutted by.

'Well, she wasn't very friendly,' I huffed.

Stan flopped down beside me, his tongue hanging out as he panted for breath. 'Oh, *her*,' he said, nodding his head. 'That's Maria Fernanda. She's a Chihuahua. She's not ignoring you – she's Mexican so she hardly speaks a word of English. She's alright when you get to know her, though.'

'I see,' I said, even though I didn't, not really.

Stan held a paw to his mouth and let out an ear-splitting whistle. Maria turned and waved over to him fondly. She signalled with her paw for him to give her a call.

'I'll ring soon, I promise,' Stan said, giving her a wink. It made Maria blush from her pretty little face right down to the tips of her toes.

'Like I said, you'll get to meet all walks of life here. Even some pretty ladies.' Stan grinned.

'Is she your girlfriend?' I asked, but Stan wasn't listening, instead, he was looking over my shoulder.

'Hang onto your boots, little fella! Here comes Winston.'

I turned my head to see a huge, white, dumpy-looking dog bounding over towards us.

'Blimey, he's massive!' I gasped. 'What sort of dog is he?'

'A bulldog,' Stan whispered out of the side of his mouth. 'But don't worry, his bark is worse than his bite. Now then, Winston,' he called out. 'How are you, old chap?'

'Ooh, not bad, me old china plate! Mustn't grumble anyway,' he replied in a cockney accent. 'Whatcha, who's this dustbin lid 'ere then?' he said, looking down at me.

I gulped nervously because I felt very small indeed.

'Winston,' said Stan, clearing his throat. 'I'd like to introduce my friend Dez. He's new to the area, just moved in around the corner.'

'Alright, me old sparrow,' Winston grinned, grabbing my paw in a firm, meaty grasp, giving it a shake.

'Oh no, sir! I'm not a sparrow, I'm a Labrador,' I tried to explain. 'And one day, I hope to become a guide dog.'

Winston turned to look at Stan and then back at me. He lifted his back paw and gave his right ear a good old scratch.

'Are you having a bubble bath?' He smirked, letting out an enormous roar of laughter. 'Aw, don't, I think I'm gonna wet me Alan Whicker's!'

'What?'

Stan chuckled when he saw the look on my face. 'Bubble bath – laugh. Alan Whicker's – knickers! OK?'

I looked down. 'But he's not wearing any Alan Whick... I mean, knickers.'

The two of them fell about laughing.

'I'll tell you summat for nuffink. He's Barney Rubble!' Winston howled, pointing down at me.

'Barney Rubble?' I said, turning to Stan for a translation.

'Barney Rubble – trouble!'

Stan howled.

The English bulldog was laughing so much that he let out a loud fart!

PARP!

'Oops, sorry about that!' He chuckled, waving a paw behind his bum to get rid of the smell. 'It's just I'm so Mork & Mindy (windy) that I've let out a raspberry tart (fart)!'

But I was still confused why Winston had called me a sparrow.

'No!' Stan gasped, wiping a tear from his eye. 'He knows you're not a bird, it's just what they say, down in London. Winston's a cockney, you see, so he talks in what they call Rhyming Slang – it's what they do down in London, isn't it, Winston?'

Winston shook his head, but he was still laughing.

'*London!*' I gasped. 'Do you know the Queen?'

Winston stopped giggling. 'Her Maj?' he said, standing up straight. 'Gawd bless her!' Suddenly he looked so serious that I half-expected him to salute or something. 'Nah, listen to me, me old china,' he said, wrapping a kindly paw around my shoulder. 'I don't know the old baked bean.'

'Queen?' I butted in, finally cottoning on to his strange way of rhyming two words together to form one.

He nodded and continued: 'Yep, I don't know the baked bean, but I do know someone who's friends with her corgis and they're right little lords and ladies, so I don't reckon they'd knock around with an old fella like me.'

Winston had just started telling me about the corgis when an elderly lady called his name.

'Uh-oh, better go! It's 'er indoors, wants me back. I better hurry otherwise she'll Darby and Joan – that's moan, kid,' he said, prodding me lightly against my chest. 'Anyway,' he added, rising to his feet. 'I'll catch you later, china plate (mate),' he said, turning to Stan, patting him on the shoulder.

'As for you, Dez, well, you might still have a lot to learn but you're a good 'un, I can tell.'

With that, Winston turned and left.

'He seemed nice,' I said, as we watched him disappear along the grass.

'Yeah, he's kind of in charge here but he's a hard man to please. If he didn't like you, he'd soon let you know, but I reckon you did okay there.'

'Did I?'

Moments later, I heard my own name being called.

'Looks like it's time to go,' said Stan, getting up to his feet.

'Same time tomorrow?' I asked hopefully.

'You betcha, kid!'

With that, we strolled out of the park, along the street and back home, where dinner was waiting.

As I snuggled down later that evening on Niki's lap, I knew everything would be absolutely fine. Maria the Mexican and Winston were just so different from anyone I'd ever met before and now I couldn't wait to make more friends and start the rest of my new life.

CHAPTER 5

WATER PUP

The following day, it was much warmer, almost too hot for running, but I still gave it my best shot. Stan and I were wandering through the park, with Lisa and Niki close behind, when we saw a bright yellow van pull in through the big main gates. It trundled along the path and parked up at the edge of the slides and swings where the children were playing.

'I didn't think cars were allowed in here?' I said.

'It's not a car, it's a van – an ice-cream van,' Stan explained.

'What's ice cream?' I asked, a little bewildered.

Stan licked his lips as he tried to describe it in all its glory. 'Well, it's a bit like a pudding. It's a lovely, sweet cream, which is ice-cold. That's where it gets its name from, ice cream... and it's utterly delicious.'

'So you think if we asked nicely the man might let us have an ice cream?' I suggested, 'Because I'd love to try one.'

Suddenly, Stan started to choke. 'Mista Sunshine?' he spluttered. 'You've got to be kidding! He's the most miserable, meanest man there is.'

'Er, but he's called Mista Sunshine?'

'Yep, I know. Ironic, isn't it? Nope, there's no chance he'd give you an ice cream, lolly or even a bowl of water. You see, he doesn't like dogs, or parks. To be honest, he doesn't like kids, or even ice cream.'

'So why does he sell it, if he doesn't like it?'

Stan shrugged his shoulders. 'Search me.'

As I watched the children form a queue at Mista Sunshine's ice-cream van, someone shouted over.

'Excuse me,' the voice called.

We both turned to see a white, furry, blue-eyed husky strolling over towards us.

'Can we help you?' Stan asked politely.

'Oh, you wouldn't be a dear, would you, and tell me where I could pick up a nice cup of hot tea?'

Stan paused for a moment and scratched his head with his back leg. 'Er, well, there's a cafe around the other side of the park, near the lake,' he said, gesturing over towards it. 'You might be able to get one there. I know they sell them to humans, but I'm not so sure about, er, dogs, because tea isn't supposed to be good for us.'

'Oh, thank you *so* much,' the husky replied, shivering a little. 'It's just that I'm so very cold and I need a little something to warm me up. It's the weather, you see, isn't it dreadful?'

I squinted against the sunlight as I looked up at the sun perched in a cloudless blue sky. It was a lovely, warm summer's day.

'But it's not cold. Look how many children are queuing up to buy ice cream. It's red hot!'

'Brrr, it isn't!' the husky disagreed, rubbing her paws together. 'I'm absolutely freezing. I only wish I had thicker fur, and then maybe I'd feel a little bit warmer.'

Stan looked at me and back at the husky. Her fur was

so thick, it looked as though she'd been rolled in a plump white duvet.

'Er, but you're a husky. Aren't you supposed to like the cold?' he asked.

At this the husky threw back her head and began to laugh.

'Oh no, I HATE the cold! If I could, I'd live somewhere hot and sunny, somewhere like Jamaica, somewhere there's always sun. That's why I need a hot drink. I need something to take the chill away.'

'So you don't like ice cream?' I guessed correctly.

'I HATE ice cream! Why anyone would ever want to eat something so cold, well, it's beyond me. Anyway, toodle pip, chaps,' she said, shaking all four feet. 'Must dash, my paws feel like blocks of ice!'

'She's a bit bonkers, that one,' said Stan, circling a paw at the side of his head.

'Yeah, I reckon she needs some loop the loop.' I replied in a cockney accent.

'Eh?'

'Soup!'

Stan sniggered.

'*Don't*, you're beginning to sound like Winston!'

Stan and I talked long into the afternoon, but because it was so warm, we found a shady spot under the shadow of some tall trees.

'Look at those humans, sunning themselves,' he remarked. 'I don't know how they can stand it in this heat!'

He panted. His long pink tongue dangled out of the

corner of his mouth. I did the same. It was the only way to feel cooler, because unlike humans, we dogs sweat through our paws and cool ourselves using our tongues, which is why they are always hanging out!

'So,' Stan said, breaking the silence. 'Where are you going on your holidays?'

I shrugged my shoulders. 'Not sure, I heard Niki telling Jon, my puppy-walker dad, about it. All I know is that we're going camping with some friends of theirs, and they've got a dog called Misty.'

'Ooh, potential girlfriend material?' Stan said, nudging me with his elbow.

'No, nothing like that! I think she's two, so she's old enough to be my mum, but it'd be nice to make a new friend. I hope she likes running, otherwise I'm going to be really bored.'

A week or so later, Niki and John packed up the car to go on my first holiday. I jumped happily into the back of it, as the kids piled onto the back seat. The car was full to bursting and so was I – with excitement. I wondered what camping would be like.

'You'll love Misty,' Niki called from the front seat. 'And I'm sure she's going to love you, Dez.'

I wagged my tail happily. A holiday and a new friend, I could hardly wait! But I did worry a little bit.

What if Misty was old and didn't want to run around? Then I'd be really bored.

If I thought I'd be bored with Misty, then I was wrong because she had twice as much energy as me. Short and sandy brown in colour, she had a grey black tail which never stopped wagging.

'Come on, slow coach!' she laughed as we ran around the campsite. The grass felt lovely, cool and fresh against the pads of my paws, but I was out of breath just trying to keep up.

'Hang on, I'm coming,' I panted, running as fast as my little legs would carry me.

Misty was a girl border Staffie-cross, who loved messing around.

'So, do you want to play ball?' she said.

'What's a ball?' I asked, a little confused.

'It's a round, bouncy thing, which humans throw. They throw them, we chase them. So, do you wanna play?'

'Oh, you mean a BALL!' I exclaimed, 'Is that what they're called?'

'Yeah, but why do you say it like that?' Misty asked, cocking her head slightly to one side.

'Because guide dogs aren't allowed to play with balls.'

'Why not? Balls are fun, and so are sticks. Do you play with sticks?'

'No, I'm not allowed to play with them either,' I said, shaking my head sadly, although I didn't tell her I didn't even know what sticks were.

'What, no balls or sticks? Sheesh, it must be rubbish being a guide dog!'

'No, it's not that. We're supposed to concentrate when we're working, so we're not allowed to chase after things like balls just in case they distract us when we're older.'

'Well, I think that sounds boring,' Misty concluded, looking over at me with pity. 'Listen, kid, I've got a secret ball stashed away in a corner over there. Why don't we go and play with it?'

'Er,' I said, checking slyly over my shoulder for Niki, but she was busy talking to Sue, Misty's owner. 'Okay, but only if we're quick because I don't want to get into trouble.'

Misty smirked and started making bird noises.

'Chicken,' she clucked, flapping her paws, making fun of me.

'Am *not*!' I said, sticking out my tongue at her.

'Come on then, follow me.'

I followed Misty to a corner of the campsite, where she

parted some long grass with her front paw. Sure enough, when she pulled it back, there it was – an old, discoloured tennis ball.

'Catch!' she whooped.

Misty jumped up with the ball in her mouth. She threw it high in the air, and punched it with one paw. I ran to fetch it, so she did it again and again until I felt dizzy and breathless. After a while, Misty got bored and wanted to rest but I'd only just got started.

'Come on,' I said, all revved up like a car engine, 'don't stop now!'

I jumped on her neck, giving her a puppy nip to get her to move.

'But Dez, I'm exhausted!' she yawned.

'Tomorrow then, will you come and play tomorrow?' I begged, my tail swishing behind me frantically.

'Okay, I'll call for you, first thing.'

That afternoon when we got back to the tent I was still full of energy. I was just wondering what to do when I caught the scent of a delicious aroma in the breeze.

What was it?

I lifted my head and sniffed some more. Whatever it was, it was definitely coming from the tent next door. I got up and furtively sniffed around the door.

Yep, it was definitely coming from in there. But what was it?

I knew I shouldn't, but grabbing the zip between my teeth, I unzipped the door and tiptoed into the stranger's tent.

Now, let me see, I thought, trying to concentrate. I lifted my head and sniffed some more. It was definitely coming over from the corner and I was certain it was sweets. *Someone had sweets in their rucksack!* I began to feel a little giddy.

Using my paws, I undid the rucksack and pushed my head inside so I could snuffle some more. I heard a paper bag rustle and shoved my snout into it. Opening my mouth, I was just about to take a bite when...

'DEZ! What on earth are you doing?'

It was Niki.

Uh-oh! I stood up sharply because I'd been caught red-handed, or red-pawed.

'Dez, what on earth... come here! You must never, ever go in other people's tents,' Niki scolded.

I looked up, but I had tell-tale sugar caked around my mouth. It made Niki gasp.

'But sweets and STEALING! Oh, Dez, what on earth am I going to do with you?' she sighed.

Niki was right, stealing was wrong. I knew that but I loved sweets so much.

In the end, she tied me to a stick outside the tent to keep me from mischief and to stop me from sneaking into any more tents.

'You've got to learn, Dez. Stealing is wrong,' Niki insisted.

I sighed and slumped sadly to the ground.

Sorry, Niki, I whimpered, clambering to my feet as she passed by again later that afternoon.

'Oh, Dez,' she sighed, ruffling the fur lovingly on the top of my head. 'The thing is, if I can't teach you right from wrong, then they won't take you as a guide dog.'

I looked up at her, my eyes beginning to water.

'Come on,' she said, untying the rope. 'I'll let you off, but only if you promise to behave yourself.'

I promise! I barked happily.

But Niki was right: if I wanted to make the grade as a guide dog then I was going to have to behave myself, so that's what I tried to do.

The following morning, Misty called by with her owners, Sue and Paul.

'Morning!' she cried in a bright and cheerful voice. 'Do you want to go and explore?'

'I'd love to,' I said, scampering to my feet.

We walked for ages. Once the humans had let us off our leads, Misty and I went exploring in the woods. As I followed, I noticed she seemed to be searching for something.

'What have you lost?' I asked.

'Nothing,' she explained, sniffing the ground. 'I'm looking for sticks.'

I scratched my head.

'You know what sticks are, right?' she said, suddenly stopping in her tracks.

'Yeah, course I do,' I fibbed.

But I didn't, not really.

'Well,' she said, sticking her nose back down to the ground. 'If you see any good ones, give me a shout.'

'Oh, I will!' I replied, as I stuck my nose against a pile of leaves and tried to copy what she was doing. I walked along, sniffing along the ground like a doggy hoover, and then my head suddenly hit something: a little brown body and four skinny legs were standing right in front of me.

'You don't know what sticks are, do you?'

Misty had guessed correctly.

'Yes, I do!' I protested, but I knew I'd been found out. 'Erm, erm, they're...'

But my voice stammered as I tried my best to think of something to say.

'Look, Dez, if you don't know, then just say. I'm not going to laugh or make fun. But you mustn't lie to me, not ever. Understand?'

I nodded my head glumly because now I felt stupid.

'Yes, I understand.'

Misty beckoned me further into the woods as she began to explain what sticks were. 'They're brown, sticky things attached to trees,' she told me, while giving me a guided tour. Suddenly she stopped and lifted her head. 'Look up there!' She gestured upwards with her nose to a branch in the tree above.

'But that's a branch.'

'Yeah, but branches get broken up and then they turn into sticks,' she explained.

Misty was clearly on the trail of one as her nose hovered along the ground. A few seconds later, she turned to me with a huge piece of branch wedged in her mouth. It gave her a wooden smile.

'Scheee, this isss wha I mea...nnn,' she drooled, as she clamped it tight in her jaw.

'But what can you do with a stick?' I asked.

Misty dropped it to the ground.

'What *can't* you do? You can throw it, like this,' she said, grabbing one end, throwing it up in the air. 'You can hide it, bury it, or you can snap it in half with your teeth like this.'

She panted, crunching it between her front canines.

CRUNCH!

The stick split clean in half.

'Here, you have that bit,' she said, nudging it towards me.

'Oh, no! We're not allowed to play with balls or sticks, only toys.'

Misty sighed and shook her head.

'Well, I think it's a stupid rule because I love sticks, they're the best!'

'But aren't they meant to be dangerous, and what if you get splinters in your tongue?'

Misty stopped chewing. 'What? Blimey, Dez, you're a right little Goody Two-Shoes, aren't you? Next, you'll be telling me you're not allowed to swim.'

My face flushed bright red.

'Well, erm, I'm not allowed to go in water, if that's what you mean. It's another rule and...'

Misty held up her paw to stop me. 'Good grief! Aren't you allowed to have any fun? What's the matter, Dezzy boy, are you frightened? Is that what it is? Are you scared of dipping your paw in the pond, hmm?'

I shook my head.

'Of course not, I'm braver than you!'

'Bet you're not!'

'*Am*,' I argued.

'Okay then, superdog! Come on, let's see how good you are. Let's go for a swim!' Misty suggested, her eyes glistening with excitement.

'But I haven't brought my... I mean...' I stammered.

'What, haven't you brought your pink bikini, is that it? Diddums!' she teased, sticking out her bottom lip.

I looked over my shoulder. My puppy walkers were close behind with Misty's family.

'Come on, I dare you!' She panted, running off towards the lake. 'Anyway,' she called back, 'it'll be fuuuuunnnn!' Her voice trailed as she disappeared towards the water's edge.

'Okay, coming!' I barked, trying to catch her up.

'*Dez!*' I heard Niki's voice call from behind, but once I'd started running, I couldn't stop. Instead I focused on Misty, who'd already jumped into the water.

'This is so much fun!' she giggled, splashing with her paws.

'Geronimo...' I howled, as I shut my eyes and ran. As my paws left the ground, I sailed high into the air and that's when I remembered... I COULDN'T SWIM!

'*Dez!*' Niki's voice called in a panic.

SPLASH!

The water swallowed me whole as it whooshed up and over the top of my head. I tried to open my eyes, but the dirty lake stung against them, making everything blurred.

'GLUG, GLUG,' I spluttered. I tried to move my arms around and copy Misty, but it wasn't easy. Then I noticed her face change as she watched me struggle to keep my head above water.

'You can swim, can't you?' she barked loudly across the water.

'No, no! GLUG! NO!' I coughed.

'But *all* dogs can swim! Can't you do the doggy paddle?'

'What's... GLUG. COUGH. SPLUTTER. What's the doggy paddle?'

Everything went dark as Misty swam over to save me. I felt a hand against my collar and then the sensation of being pulled upwards as Harry, Niki's youngest son (besides me) fished me out, coughing and spluttering.

'Dez, what on earth...?' Niki sighed as she wrapped me up in a dry towel. I was shivering with both cold and shock.

'Sorry, Niki,' I whined.

'What on earth were you thinking? You could have drowned!'

Niki didn't tell me off because she was worried I'd hurt myself. It took me a few hours, but eventually I began to thaw out. I was just starting to get warm when I heard two voices outside the tent – it was Sue and Misty.

'Dez!' Misty said, coming inside to give me a cuddle. 'I'm sorry, I thought you could swim.'

'So did I! I forgot I couldn't, and by the time I'd remembered it was too late,' I said, shuddering.

'Oh, Dez! Don't worry, I can teach you, if you like. We could go paddling; build it up slowly. You'll need to learn one day, so it may as well be now.'

After my near-death experience, I was a little scared to

dip a paw in the water, but Misty taught me in stages until soon I was able to swim without water wings.

'Thanks, Misty!' I giggled, because I now realised just how much fun it could be.

'You're welcome. We'll make a guide dog out of you yet!'

'Yeah,' I said, splashing her in the face, 'just don't tell them I've played with balls and sticks, otherwise they'll throw me out!'

The rest of the week passed by without incident and all too soon the holiday was at an end. I'd had such a brilliant time.

'See you next year?' Misty asked me.

'Definitely!' I woofed.

CHAPTER 6

FAST FOOD

'So, how was your holiday?' Stan asked as we strolled in the park, a few days later.

'Erm, well, it was, hmm, you know, a little eventful!' I replied.

'Huh?' Stan replied, giving me a sideways glance. 'Why's that?'

I explained all about the sticks, balls and breaking into the tent for sweets. Then I told him about the lake Misty and I had splashed about in.

'...and I almost drowned! But Harry saved me. Then Misty taught me how to swim.'

Stan shook his head: 'Sounds like you had quite an adventure. As for Misty, well, she sounds like quite a gal!' He grinned. 'I think you'll have to introduce me sometime.'

We walked around the park, with Stan filling me in on what I'd missed while I'd been away.

'Winston was asking about you, me old china plate!' he chuckled, trying to mimic the bulldog's accent.

'Was he?'

'Yeah, he said, "Where's the old bin lid?" – kid, meaning you. Proper smart he looked too. He was wearing his new Union Jack shirt, or "Dickie Dirt", as he called it.'

At this I sniggered. I could imagine Winston proud and patriotic, dressed in the English flag.

'I love Winston – he's so funny, the way he talks.'

'He is, son, he is,' Stan agreed.

Moments later, he looked up.

'Hey, have I introduced you to Willow?'

'Er, no, I don't think so.'

'Well, don't look now, but here she comes.'

'Hi boys,' Willow said, striding towards us like a four-legged supermodel. She sashayed slightly and then swivelled towards Stan, fluttering her long, black eyelashes. 'Who's your little friend, then?' she asked, looking down at me from the top of her impossibly long legs.

Willow was a beautiful, if not slightly skinny, tall grey-hound. It was obvious she liked Stan by the way she was gazing at him adoringly.

'Oh, Willow, meet Dez. He's training to become a guide dog.'

'Ooh,' Willow cooed, with a paw to her chest, her eyelashes fluttering twice as fast, 'I *love* a dog in uniform! So, have you started training?'

'No, not yet – I've got another six months before I go back to the guide-dog training centre.'

Willow listened intently; she almost seemed impressed. 'I was once a professional, you know,' she chipped in.

'Really? What did you do?'

Willow's eyes misted over as she began to explain. 'I was an athlete – a runner. I was faster than Usain Bolt – a champion in my day, but...' her voice tailed off, as she looked down sadly, '...I'm afraid I can no longer compete.'

'Why not?'

'Because I've let myself go, I've put on a little weight. I'm a bit... fat,' she said, whispering the last word.

'FAT?!' I exclaimed.

'Shush!' Willow screeched, looking round to check no one had heard me.

'But you're not fat!' I insisted.

Tall and elegant, like a giraffe, she was slim, so slim that you could see her ribs.

'That's what I've been trying to tell her,' Stan interrupted. 'But she won't listen.'

'Do you not think so?' Willow murmured.

'No, not at all! If anything, I think you're a bit skinny.'

'Really?' she gasped. 'But... but don't you think my bum looks big?'

She turned around for me to take a look.

'Nope!'

'And my ankles, don't they look a little bit swollen to you?' I shook my head.

'What about my belly? Don't you think I look a bit podgy?' she asked, squidging a tiny ripple of skin between her paws.

'No,' I insisted. 'If anything, you look like you could do with a good meal! Listen, life is too short to worry about your weight, you should just relax and enjoy yourself.'

Willow's eyes blinked back tears of relief. 'You're so kind, Dez. I think that's the nicest thing anyone ever said to me.'

I laughed. 'Maybe that's because I love my food a little too much,' I chuckled, tapping my big, round tum. 'If I could get my hands on one of those ice creams or anything sweet, then I'd be one happy pup!'

Stan and Willow laughed as I licked my lips dreamily.

'Hmmm,' I sighed, lost in my fantasy.

Despite the joke, my wish came sooner than I thought. The following day, I was in the park, only this time Stan wasn't with me. He was at the dog groomer's, having a much-needed haircut. He didn't say it, but I think he was smartening himself up for Willow, because he'd asked her out on a dinner date. So, I was all alone and to be honest, without my best pal I was a little bit bored. Teatime was ages away and I was starving hungry. Niki had let me off the lead, but she was busy talking when I spotted something out of the corner of my eye: a huge pile of unattended sandwiches. The bread looked soft, white and fluffy – the perfect snack to sink my teeth into. Although I didn't know what fillings they had, they looked delicious. I glanced over one shoulder, and saw that Niki wasn't watching. Then I looked back at the picnic sandwiches: they were sitting on a plastic plate in the middle of a tartan blanket, surrounded by some cups of orange squash. I glanced around, once more.

Nope, they've been left all alone. Maybe they wouldn't miss a few little sandwiches, I reasoned, my mouth drooling.

I ran towards them. My belly was rumbling, and I was desperate to grab just one sandwich. I ran faster and faster as I heard Niki's voice calling me from a distance. 'Dez... Oh, noooooo!' her voice trailed as I kept the sandwiches firmly in my sight.

With a deft flick of my head, I picked up as many sandwiches as I could grab from the top of the pile. With a wedge of them dangling from my mouth, I dashed over to the hedge, where I tried to hide. I knew it was wrong, but sometimes my belly just took over. As I gobbled them down one by one, I couldn't believe how delicious they tasted. They were filled with some sticky red stuff I'd never had before. It was so scrumptious that I craved more. As I chewed away, I spotted a figure running towards me: it was Niki, and she looked none too happy.

Uh-oh! I thought, dipping my head guiltily. *I'm in trouble... again!*

'No, Dez, that's naughty!' Niki scolded.

I thought she'd try and grab the last of my stolen sandwiches, so I wolfed it down in one mouthful.

GULP!

But Niki seemed more disappointed than angry, which made me feel worse. With my belly full, I stood there with my head dipped as she told me off.

'Well, I suppose I'll have to go over and apologise to those poor people,' she sighed. 'You do realise, you've ruined their picnic!'

Niki was right, of course. I cocked my head to one side so that I could look behind her legs. The picnicking family didn't look very happy at having their sandwiches stolen by a greedy pup. It made me feel really bad. I was worried they'd tell Guide Dogs, and then I'd get into some real trouble.

'Come on, you're going to come over with me and say sorry,' she said, clipping my lead on. As I stood with my eyes cast guiltily to the ground, Niki apologised on my behalf. I continued to hang my Labrador head in shame as I licked the remains of the gorgeous sticky-sweet mixture from my mouth.

It really did taste delicious, I thought, my mind wandering.

'I'm *so* sorry,' Niki apologised to the man, his wife and two children. 'He's a, erm, guide dog in training. I don't know what came over him. I mean, he's usually so good...'

But the man had heard enough. 'My children were really looking forward to those strawberry jam sandwiches,' he said, interrupting her.

Mmmmmmmm! I thought, my tongue slurping the outside of my mouth. *Strawberry jam, that's what it's called!*

Strawberry jam had just become my new favourite food! It tasted so much better than plain old boring dog biscuits. I tried to remember the name 'strawberry' as Niki continued:

'...so... please, let me give your children some money for ice cream, it's the very least I can do,' she said, taking her purse out of her bag.

Later that evening, when she'd recounted the whole sorry tale to the rest of the family, they turned to look at me in horror.

'Dez? You mean he's a sandwich thief!' Molly gasped.

''Fraid so.' Niki nodded, as she stacked up plates in the dishwasher.

I was worried because I'd got into trouble over the sandwiches, but now I'd tasted strawberries, it was all I could think of. A few days later, the sun was shining so we headed out in the car for a day at the seaside. By the time we'd arrived, the beach was packed. The golden sand felt soft and slippy, but lovely and warm beneath my four paws. Molly was busy pulling out towels from a bag with Niki. I was just looking towards the sea when my Labrador nose detected a sweet scent blowing in the breeze. I glanced all around – it smelled exactly the same as the delicious sandwiches I'd snaffled in the park. My head spun, taking in the crowded beach and all the people. I looked at what food they were eating.

SNIFF...

Hmmmm, my mouth drooled. *Fish and chips, with lashings of salt and vinegar, delicious!*

But it wasn't that (even though they smelt really good). I lifted my head and tried to concentrate.

SNIFF...

Suntan lotion? No, I thought, shaking my head, *it definitely wasn't that*. So I tried again. *Strawberry, wasn't that what the picnic man had called it? Hmmm, yes, I could certainly smell strawberries! But where was the delicious aroma coming from?*

My eyes flicked from one family to the next, but there wasn't a sandwich in sight. I sniffed the air some more, and that's when I spotted them – a punnet of red, heart-shaped pieces of fruit on a blanket between two ladies.

Ah, so that's what strawberries look like!

I checked where Niki was, but she was still busy with Molly and the towels, so I edged closer and gave the air a second, cursory sniff.

Yep, they were definitely strawberries! I decided.

I turned around. Molly and Niki were unrolling towels, while Jon and the boys had gone for a quick splash about in the sea. I saw my chance. Now, I knew I shouldn't, because stealing was wrong, but my belly rumbled and the strawberries looked so delicious. Although I knew I'd get into even more trouble, once again I allowed my belly to rule my head.

'*Geronimo!*' I barked, as I charged full pelt towards two women and the delicious strawberries.

Hurry up! I panicked. I noticed one of the women take a strawberry from the top. Out of breath and panting, I didn't care. I charged straight through the middle of them, grabbing a mouthful of fruit as I dashed by in a doggy blur.

'NOM, NOM, NOM...' I chomped. My mouth was so stuffed full of strawberries that the red juice was streaming out of the front of it.

'*Dez!*' Molly shrieked.

'Oh no, *not* again!' Niki sighed.

Jon was looking towards me, scratching his head in bewilderment.

'What the...?' he began to say, but I couldn't hear the rest because his voice was blown away by the sea breeze.

Of course, I was told off again, but what they didn't understand was now I'd got a taste for strawberries I couldn't help myself – they were my favourite food in the whole world. I wasn't supposed to eat them because I was a dog, and not just a guide dog, but a doggy strawberry thief too!

CHAPTER 7

THE WESTIE SISTERS

'So,' said Stan, 'I heard about you stealing strawberries.' He arched an eyebrow as he gazed down at me disapprovingly.

'Er, who told you?'

'No one, it's the talk of the park. Who would've thought it, eh? Dez the strawberry thief!'

'Are you talking about the sandwiches or the day out at the beach?' I asked.

'What? You mean you've done it twice!'

'Er...' I cast my eyes down guiltily.

Stan began to tut.

'Dez, my son, I honestly thought you were better than that!'

My face blushed as I glanced up at him.

'Sorry, Stan.'

'I should think so! I thought you were a decent kid, not a

common...' Stan stopped mid-sentence, lifted his head and pricked his ears up in the air. ''Ere, can you hear that?'

I tried to listen, but my big ears flapped around and got in the way.

'Hear what?'

'Shush!' said Stan, putting a paw to his lips. 'Listen, it sounds like there's a dog in pain.' He tilted his head and turned both ears like mini antennae to try and pick up the noise. 'There it goes again, that's definitely a dog in pain.'

I flipped one of my ears over the top of my head so I could hear what he could.

'I heard it too! It's coming from over there, near those bushes,' I said, pointing over to them. 'Come on, let's go. Someone must be trapped!'

Stan and I ran as fast as we could over towards the bushes. Then I stopped and swung my head so both ears flapped and landed on top of my head. I signalled for Stan to be quiet, so we could work out where the noise was coming from.

'Whaaaa, Wha, Whahhhhh, Wha, Wha, Wahhhhh! Bum bum bum, dum de dummm...' the voice whined.

'Whatever do you think it is?' I asked.

'I dunno. But it could be a trapped dog, so we have to act fast!'

Charging through the bushes into a small clearing, I braced myself for something horrible – a dog with its leg broken, or something even worse. Instead we found two little Westies. One was standing on top of a small rock, posing. She had one paw clutched to her chest, making the dreadful din, while the other was crouched on the floor, both paws over her ears.

'Make her stop... Purlease, just make her stop!' the second one cried, begging for mercy.

'Who is she?' I shouted, clamping my ears against my head to stop the dreadful noise from seeping in.

The little Westie looked up at me, exasperated.

'She's my sister, pet. She's called Kilty.'

'Milty?' I shouted.

'No, KILTY!' she hollered over the awful din.

'Oh, sorry,' I replied, nodding my head to show I'd understood.

'But what's wrong with her? I mean, is she in pain?' asked Stan, trying to pin down the tips of both ears to his head.

'No man, she thinks she's a singer,' Bonnie cried.

'A SINGER?' Stan and I chorused in surprise.

'Aye, a singer! But she's got an awful voice.'

Suddenly, Kilty stopped singing and the three of us sighed with relief.

'I think you'll find I *am* a singer, Bonnie, man,' she said, fixing her sister with a steely glare.

Bonnie shrugged her shoulders.

'See what I mean? She's clearly disillusioned. She couldn't carry a tune, even if it was in a wheelbarrow.'

Just then the sisters began to argue.

'Can!'

'Can't!'

'Can!'

'Can't!'

Stan put a paw up to halt them.

'Listen, ladies, I think we'd better pause for a moment and do the introductions. My name is Stan,' he said, patting a paw against the fur on his chest, 'and this...' he said, stretching out his other paw, '...is my good friend, Dez.'

'Hiya,' Bonnie said, smiling.

'Pleased to meet you,' Kilty answered, doing a theatrical curtsey on top of the rock, which she'd pretended was a stage.

Bonnie rolled her eyes and groaned. 'Well, as you've probably worked out, I'm Bonnie, and this,' she said, nudging her head over towards where her sister was standing, 'is her ladyship, Kilty.'

'Honoured, I'm sure,' Kilty said, batting her eyelashes sweetly.

I felt myself go red as I searched for the right words.

'So... erm... you're a singer then, Kilty?' I mumbled.

'I am, pet!' She beamed. 'And whatever you do, don't forget this face, because one day, I'm gonna be a star! One night, you'll see me on telly.'

Bonnie shook her head in disbelief.

'In ya dreams,' she muttered under her breath, but loud enough for Stan and me to hear.

'Now, the most important thing is, when you're a singer like me,' Kilty said, hopping down daintily from her rock, 'is to try and preserve your voice. Now,' she added, suddenly sounding posh, peering all around her. 'Oh, yes, over here! That's perfect.' She smiled, lining herself up in front of a puddle. 'Now then, every day I look in the mirror and practise my VOWELS...' she explained, pronouncing each letter of the word.

Suddenly, she dropped the posh accent.

'Dez, pet, come over here and join us...' she said, waving a paw, beckoning me over.

'But why do you both keep calling us "pet"?' I asked, a little confused.

'It's because we're from Newcastle, pet,' Bonnie explained, her eyes widening as she stood up with pride. 'It's only the greatest city in the whole wide world!'

Kilty grabbed my shoulder and beamed at me, her eyes glistening with excitement. 'And it's where Cheryl Cole's from – well, Cheryl whatever she's called now she's got married again. Anyway, it's where our Cheryl's from. And one day, I'm gonna be just like her.'

Kilty lifted up her paw and swept it across, as though spelling out the words in mid-air. 'KILTY WATSON, I can just see it now – my name in big letters, in theatres and on the telly. It's Kilty, by the way,' she said, breaking off for a moment, 'NOT Milty. And I'll be great, just like our Cheryl. We could duet together and maybe one day I might even get to sing with Harry Styles!' she added, squealing with delight.

Bonnie sniggered as Kilty dipped her head bashfully.

'Harry who?' I asked.

'HARRY STYLES, One Deeee,' she said, showing her teeth and emphasising the 'D'. 'Don't tell me you don't know! Don't tell me you've never heard of One Direction!'

I shrugged. Kilty turned away in disgust, as though she'd

given up all hope. She looked at her glowing white reflection in the puddle.

'A.E.I.O.U.,' she said.

As she did so, the muscles in her mouth and neck stretched like Plasticine.

'What's she doing?' I asked, looking over towards Bonnie.

'She's practising her vowels – she thinks they help with her voice, and keep her, erm, young-looking...'

'I *am* young!' Kilty tutted, as she turned sharply on all four paws. 'Besides, you're only jealous, just because ya weren't blessed with a voice as pure as mine.'

'I wouldn't call it pure, more poor,' Bonnie grumbled in a low murmur.

'What did she say?' Kilty demanded.

'Dunno.' I shrugged.

'Sorry, didn't catch it,' Stan lied, getting to his feet. 'Anyway, ladies, my friend and I really must dash. You know, things to do, people to meet.'

'Nice to meet ya both,' Kilty called cheerfully, looking over the top of her sister's head. With her snub black shiny nose, and cute little button eyes, she really was one of the prettiest Westies I'd ever seen.

Maybe she already was a star? I'd never seen X Factor, so I couldn't be sure. Maybe Kilty was already the real deal?
Slowly, I started to feel a little star-struck.

'Y... y... you too,' I said, suddenly starting to flush a little. Kilty's beauty was beginning to make me a little hot under the collar. 'And you know I'll look out for you...'

'Eh?' she said, looking up at me.

'On X *Factor*,' I said, crossing my front paws to show her. It made her chuckle.

'You will that, me and Harry! I'll have to nudge our Cheryl out the way, though,' she giggled, pretending to push Bonnie over with her elbow.

Bonnie looked up and scowled.

'See ya, lads,' Bonnie said, lifting a paw to wave. 'And next time ya hear her ladyship, remember, it's not a dog in pain, it's a wannabe Westie WAG!'

Stan howled with laughter and Bonnie joined in too, but I couldn't take my eyes off Kilty.

'Bye then, Kilty. And I hope you break a leg,' I said, waving back.

'Eh?'

'Break a leg! It's an old theatrical saying for good luck on stage,' I explained.

'Ah right, I see,' Kilty nodded. 'For a moment, I thought ya wanted me to break me leg or summat.'

'I wish you'd break your neck then at least I'd be spared ya singing,' Bonnie muttered, rolling her eyes.

'Eh?' Kilty replied.

'Nothing, I said, I hope you break a leg, and then we can all enjoy ya singing.'

A smile appeared on Kilty's face. 'Ah, right you are! Now, Bonnie, I want ya to listen to this and tell me what ya think. It's me own special version of Adele's beautiful ballad, "Someone Like You".'

As we left, Bonnie crouched back down on the ground and placed both paws on her ears.

'Bye, you two.'

She sighed as we turned to walk away.

'Poor Bonnie,' Stan remarked as we pushed back through the hedge and into the park.

'Why, I thought Kilty was rather good,' I protested.

Just then, her howls broke the silence of our surroundings.

'*Never mind, I'll find somebody like yoooouuuu, hooooo, hooooooo....*' she whined.

I turned to Stan.

'Nah, you're right,' I agreed. 'That voice could curdle milk!'

CHAPTER 8

ROGER AND MISTA SUNSHINE

Following our meeting with the Westie Sisters, Stan and I often bumped into them down the park. 'Hiya pet!' Kilty called from across the grass one day.

'Oh, hi Kilty,' I said, waving madly back at her, my face blushing.

'Er, I think someone's a little smitten with Kilty the singer...' Stan teased, giving me a sly nudge.

'No, we're just friends, that's all,' I protested, trying not to catch his eye. I hadn't realised it was that obvious.

'Now, lad, it's a big world out there and there's, erm, plenty of fish in the sea. Don't tie yourself down too young, that's my advice.'

I looked up at him, a little confused.

'But I'm not interested in fish, Stan!'

He shook his head in despair. 'No, I know that, Dez. It's

just a saying. It means you'll get to meet lots of lovely girly dogs throughout your life, so don't tie yourself down with the first one you meet.'

'Oh, right,' I replied, feeling a little foolish.

'Isn't it a glorious day?' Stan sighed, changing the subject.

I looked up at the cloudless cornflower-blue sky. It was a scorcher of a day.

'Yeah, I bet Mista Sunshine's really busy today. Hey, let's go over and take a look.'

'Okay.'

Stan and I wandered over to the other side of the park, where Mista Sunshine had parked up his van alongside the children's swings.

'Look at that queue!' gasped Stan. I followed his gaze. He was right – there must have been at least twenty children standing there, waiting to buy ice cream.

'I wish I could queue up and buy one,' I sighed. 'I've never tried ice cream before.'

My mouth watered at the thought of sweet, sticky cream melting against my tongue.

'Whatcha doing, lads?'

It was Kilty. The sisters had wandered to the other side of the park to catch us up. I felt my heart leap.

'Erm, erm...' I stuttered, a little flustered.

'Oh, nothing much,' Stan replied. 'Dez was just saying he'd love to try ice cream.'

'What's it taste like? Have you ever tried it?' I blushed.

'Oh, no, not me, pet!' Kilty said, rubbing her pink belly.

'I've got to keep myself trim, if I wanna go on telly. But our Bonnie's tried it.'

'Have you?'

Bonnie looked up at me. There was a twig tangled in a tuft of white fur on top of her head. She was a real tomboy, the total opposite of her sister.

'Ooh, I have Dez, and I have to say, it tasted delicious!' she said, licking her lips at the thought. 'Do ya know if you watch them kids over there I bet you one of them will drop one, and that's when you,' she said, nudging me against my side, 'could step in.'

'You mean I should steal one?' I asked, recalling how much trouble the strawberries had got me into. 'It's just that, er, I don't think I should...'

But Bonnie shook her head.

'No, not steal. Once food falls on the floor, humans don't want it anymore, so it just goes to waste. If you don't eat it, then it'll just melt. Anyway, that'd be your best chance.'

Stan suggested that we all go and sit under the shade of a big tree while I observed from a distance, waiting for my chance. I didn't have to wait very long. Five minutes later, a little boy who was with his mum asked for an ice cream. I watched his mother hand over some coins to the ice-cream seller. Mista Sunshine was a disgusting man. I looked on in horror as he wiped his snotty nose on the back of his hand before passing her the ice cream. The mother looked horrified, but took it from him. Just then Mista Sunshine straightened up and let out a loud fart.

PARP!

It was so loud, everyone had turned to look at him, but he didn't care. The mother shook her head in disgust. She picked up one of the bottles, which was chained to the counter to stop someone from taking it, and poured some sticky, red sauce over the top of her little boy's ice cream.

'What's that?' I asked, referring to the red stuff.

'Oh, it's just monkey's blood,' Bonnie replied.

Stan and I looked at her.

'MONKEY'S BLOOD! You mean Mista Sunshine kills monkeys for their blood, just so he can pour it on ice creams?' I gasped, holding a shocked paw against my mouth.

Bonnie and Kilty glanced at one another and burst out laughing. They rolled about on the grass, giggling, clutching their sides.

'Oh, Kilty, make him stop! I think I'm gonna wee myself,' Bonnie chortled.

'*Don't!*' Kilty replied. 'I think I already have.'

'What on earth...?' said Stan, breaking the moment. 'What's monkey's blood?'

'It's NOT actual monkey's blood, you silly billies,' Kilty explained, 'It's what we call strawberry or raspberry sauce, up in Newcastle.'

My ears picked up.

'Strawberry sauce!'

'Yeah,' said Bonnie, 'that's what kiddies put on top of their ice creams.'

I licked my lips. 'Well, why didn't you say so?'

I watched the little boy, willing him to drop the ice-cream cone. It wobbled a little as his mum handed it to him, smothered in glorious strawberry sauce. I felt my mouth water. She turned to hand his little sister an ice-lolly, and that's when it happened: another child accidentally bumped into him and the top of his ice cream plopped onto the ground.

'Go! Go! Go!' my friends screamed at me, like I was a soldier on operation.

As I ran, I watched in slow motion as the boy turned back to his mother and began to cry.

'Whaaaa!' he bawled, the empty cone in his hand.

As I looked over, I realised the ice cream had already started to melt against the warm tarmac. I ran like the wind, and within seconds I was there, standing over it, slurping up the watery mess from the floor.

'NOM, NOM, NOM!'

The ice cream tasted lovely, but the strawberry sauce was out of this world! The boy stopped crying as all the children turned to look at me – the greedy Labrador, licking ice cream up off the floor. But I didn't feel bad because I was like a doggy hoover, clearing up all the mess. The little boy began to giggle as his mother turned back to Mista Sunshine.

'He's dropped it on the ground,' she said, pointing over at me, 'and now that dog is eating it.'

I greedily slurped away at it but raised one guilty eye to look at the woman and Mista Sunshine, who was busy picking his nose. He glanced at the green bogey he'd pulled out, resting it on the tip of his finger, and then he looked down at the mother.

'So, I wondered,' she continued, 'if I could just have another little scoop to go on top of his cone...'

But Mista Sunshine wasn't listening; his face had turned bright purple. Ginger whiskers smattered across his chin were peppered with wiry grey hairs, which stood out on end, making him look even crazier. He was wearing a dirty, tea-stained string vest, which stretched across

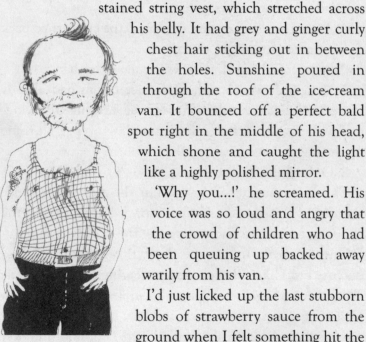

his belly. It had grey and ginger curly chest hair sticking out in between the holes. Sunshine poured in through the roof of the ice-cream van. It bounced off a perfect bald spot right in the middle of his head, which shone and caught the light like a highly polished mirror.

'Why you...!' he screamed. His voice was so loud and angry that the crowd of children who had been queuing up backed away warily from his van.

I'd just licked up the last stubborn blobs of strawberry sauce from the ground when I felt something hit the back of my head. I turned to see Mista Sunshine's brown leather shoe bounce off my head and against the grass.

'Why you dirty hound! I'll show you, eating all my ice cream!' he roared.

Panicked, I glanced over at my pals, who were calling me to run away.

'He's a nutter, Dez! Quick, run fast! Don't let him catch you,' Stan barked.

I stopped slurping and took to my heels, as Mista Sunshine climbed down from his van and gave chase. His fat belly wobbled as he ran, straining against the front of his string vest.

'If I get my hands on you, I'll squash you!' he bellowed.

Four legs are quicker than two, and although I ran as fast as I could, he was still chasing me. My heart pounded furiously as I saw his ball-shaped body bouncing behind. I was so frightened, I didn't dare look back and I didn't stop running until I'd reached the group. But as I pulled up, Stan began to giggle. Then I heard laughter coming from behind me as all the children in the park started to snigger. I looked down. Bonnie and Kilty were also doubled up with laughter and pointing at something.

'Look, Dez!' Bonnie said, urging me to turn around. 'It's Mista Sunshine. He was running so fast that his trousers have fallen down!'

As I turned my head, my mouth fell open. Mista Sunshine was standing there, pulling up his filthy black trousers. But all I could see was two thin, puny, hairy legs sticking out of the bottom of a pair of bright red spotty boxer shorts!

'Oh, he looks so funny!' Kilty giggled.

I looked over towards the queue, where the children were in fits of laughter. The little boy, whose ice cream I'd slurped down, was giggling away, along with his mother.

'It's my belt, it's snapped!' he shouted, scrunching the waistband of his trousers with both hands so they didn't drop down again. He shot me an icy glare and then turned and waddled away, red-faced, back to his van.

'Well, he wasn't very nice,' I observed.

'Told you!' Stan replied. 'He's the meanest ice-cream man for miles around. He hates sunshine, he hates kids, and he particularly hates dogs!'

'The ice cream would've just melted, but I cleaned it up for him; you'd think he'd be a little bit grateful.'

Stan shook his head. 'Doesn't matter, Dez – he wouldn't give you the steam off his cup of tea.' As he looked over my shoulder, Stan's face changed. 'Uh oh, talking of misery... don't look now, but here comes Roger.'

We all turned to see a girly Yorkshire terrier padding towards us. A pretty little thing, she was wearing a pink knitted sparkly jumper. The pink bow in her blonde fringe was so huge that it flopped down over one eye as she pranced along.

'Sorry, for a moment I thought you said her name was Roger.' I grinned, turning to Stan.

'It is,' Bonnie replied, 'and it's not a girl, it's a boy.'

My mouth fell open. 'But, er, why is she, erm, I mean he, why is he wearing that jumper? And what's with the bow?'

'It's his owner, Mavis. She's hard of hearing, so when the pet shop owner handed Roger over, she thought he'd said Rachel. Ever since then, she's been kitting him out in pink because she thinks he's a girl,' Stan whispered out of the corner of his mouth.

'No!' I gasped.

'It's true, and whatever you do, son, just don't mention the bow – he hates it! He's always trying to lose them in the park.'

Suddenly Stan stopped whispering and straightened up.

'Morning, Roger. Isn't it lovely? I was just saying to my friends here what a lovely day it w—'

'I hate t'sun,' grunted Roger, in a broad Yorkshire accent. 'It brings me out in hives. All that heat, it's too hot for a dog like me. Anyway,' he added, settling himself down in a cool spot in the shade. 'Who's the nipper?'

Stan held out his front paw and gestured over towards me. 'Roger, I'd like you to meet Dez. Dez, this is Roger.'

'How do,' he muttered.

'Hello, Miss... ster Roger,' I said, falling over my words, unable to take my eyes off the huge pink bow on top of his head.

'Go on then, lad, hurry up and take t'mickey. There's nowt you can say that hasn't already been said,' he grunted, rolling his eyes wearily.

'Whhaaa?' I said, still unsure what I could and couldn't say.

'It's t'bow, in't it? I know, I look a right state with this rubbish stuck in me hair,' he said, flicking it with a disgruntled paw. 'But what can I do, eh? Every time I lose one, she goes and buys two more.'

He sat up and turned his attention towards Stan. 'Did I tell thee I was rooting about in t'cupboard other week, you know, one under t'stairs, when I found a whole reel of pink chuffing ribbon? Reckon there's enough to make me a thousand bows!' Roger paused and sighed heavily. 'It's not just that. I found a carrier bag t'other day too – she must have about ten balls of baby-pink wool in there and two large knitting needles. Reckon I'll be wearing these horrible jumpers for the rest of my life!'

I looked over at Stan, but he didn't say a word.

'And I'll tell thee this for nothing,' Roger insisted, pointing a beautiful manicured paw up at us. His pretty little pink nails shone in the sunlight. 'If she thinks she's buying me one of those horrible bling coats with "Princess" or some other nonsense written across t'front of them, she's got another think coming!'

Kilty stifled a giggle and began to speak. 'I'll tell you what, Rog. If she buys ya one of them, pet, I'll take it off ya hands.'

'You're on!' Roger huffed, planting his ladies' paw back on the ground.

'In that case, maybe you should get one saying "Diva",' Bonnie whispered.

Roger continued to moan as the rest of us stood there and listened to his tales of woe.

'...and if I never see pink again, it'll be too soon,' he whined.

Stan's eyes had just started to glaze over when a whoosh of air blasted against the group. I looked up to see a chocolate-brown whir whiz by at lightning speed.

'What on earth was that?' I gasped, straining my eyes. It was hard to make it out, but it looked a bit like a dog. Then again, it was moving so fast that I couldn't tell.

'Oh *that*,' moaned Roger. 'That's Max. Or Mad Max, as I call him. He's a cocker spaniel. He's bonkers, they all are,' he huffed unkindly.

The brown blur shot past us again. This time it was a little slower, slow enough for me to be able to make out two dark brown eyes and a pair of curly brown ears.

'Hello, my name is Maaaaxxxxx...' The voice said, trailing behind in his wake. And then he was gone. Seconds later,

he whizzed past us again. 'Pleased to meet yyyyoooouuuu...' he hollered.

'Is he always like this?' I asked, a little startled.

'Yep,' said Roger, 'unless he's sleeping. Look out, here he comes again!'

'You must be Dez. I've heard all about yyooooouuuu...' Max's voice trailed along like the grey clouds left behind after an aeroplane has torn through the sky.

Just then another figure approached. She was small, black-and-white in colour, with a cute black patch over one eye, and her name was Marvellous Meg.

'Why do they call you Marvellous Meg?' I asked.

Meg dipped her head. 'I really don't know,' she replied modestly.

'It's because she's marvellous for putting up with that,' Roger tutted, pointing a claw at Max. The hyperactive spaniel had already run past another half a dozen times.

'He's crazy, that fella!'

'MAX!' Meg hollered. She lifted up a front paw, popped it in her mouth, curled up her tongue and let out an ear-splitting whistle. 'Where's your manners? Come here and say hello to Dez.'

Upon hearing the whistle, Max stopped dead in his tracks, his paws screeching to a halt like brakes on a car. A nanosecond later, he was by my side.

'Sorry about that, I'm Max,' he said excitedly. He took

my paw and shook it so enthusiastically that I thought it'd come out of its socket.

'I'm Dez, pleased to meet you...' I began.

'Yeah, I've heard all about you,' Max panted, butting in. 'Aren't you the one who's the strawberry thief?'

Marvellous Meg gave him a sly kick with her back leg to shut him up.

'Erm, I mean, aren't you the one who likes strawberries, or something?'

I smirked. 'Yep, guilty as charged!' I said, pulling my paw from his grasp. I held it up in mid-air as if to admit my guilt. The whole group chuckled, even miserable Roger.

'So, you've met the gang then?' Max panted.

'Yeah, I've even met Mista Sunshine. I outran him earlier.' Max grinned.

'*Sick!*' he said, slapping me so hard on my shoulder that he almost knocked me off all fours.

'Anyway, I better dash. I'm trying to improve on my time. Only fifty more laps of the park to go...' he panted. 'See ya...'

And with that he was off again, in a doggy, brown blur.

'I suppose I'd better make a move too,' I said, turning to leave. 'By the way, I'm not coming to the park tomorrow, Stan.'

'Oh, why's that?'

'Not sure, I think Niki's got something planned but I'll catch up with you later.'

Just then I heard Niki call my name across the park.

'Right, I better go. Nice meeting you, Roger and Meg, and please say goodbye to Max for me, won't you?'

'Bye, Dez,' the gang called.

I bounced over the grass towards Niki, my tail wagging high in the air with contentment. With all my new friends, I'd never felt so happy.

CHAPTER 9

CLUMSY PUP

The following morning, I decided it was time to text Violet. I wasn't sure what I should say, so I decided to be honest.

Hi Violet, itz Dez. Mum gave me your number, hope u don't mind? She told me u didn't pass the test. I'm really sorry, cos I know how that feels. Anyway, she sayz you're gonna become a buddy dog, which sounds lotz of fun. I hope u are really happy. Love you lots, Dxx

I was worried Violet would think I was gloating because she'd failed and I'd passed, but I didn't think that at all. If anything, I felt sad for her because I was worried she was unhappy. I was just thinking about everything when my mobile buzzed in my paw.

Hi Dez, it's great to hear from u! I was gonna txt u to say how sorry I was. I was really horrible and mean to u. I feel so ashamed, cos you were the kindest one of all, but I picked on u, cos I could.

I hope you'll believe me when I say I've changed. My new family are lovely & I'm really happy. I'm also looking forward to being a buddy dog, so, in a way, I'm happy for the first time in my life. I hope you can forgive me. Love your little sis, Vi xx

As soon as I read Violet's text my eyes brimmed with tears. It was all I'd ever wanted, for us to be friends. I replied immediately.

Hi Vi, I'm glad 2 hear u r happy. I am too, but I'm most happy because we are friends again. As for forgiving u, forget it, coz I already have. I love it here. I never want to leave because I've made lots of new friends. I hope you'll get 2 meet them all one day. I'm a bit scared of going back to Guide Dog School, but I've still got a bit longer before I leave. I hope I do okay. Keep in touch, won't u? Lotz of love, Dxx

I'd just pressed 'send' when my phone pinged with a response.

Don't worry about big school cos you're gonna make a brilliant guide dog. That's why I was so jealous. You are special, just like Mum said. Just wait and see. One day, you'll be top dog. Keep in touch. Bye for now. Love u lots, more than jelly tots, Vi xx

I sighed happily. I'd just tucked my mobile phone underneath my blanket when Niki walked in.

'Right, Dez, let's get your lead on, because we're going out!'

My tail wagged so hard the weight of it shook my body from side to side. Once Niki had clipped on my special guide dog lead, we were good to go.

'Whoa!' she giggled as I bolted for the front door.

For a change, Niki took me to a different park, one

that we had to drive to. Unlike before, she kept me on the lead, though.

'Right, Dez,' she said, 'let's try in here.' We strolled through some big, black metal gates into the park. 'You've never been here before, so I thought it'd be good to take you somewhere different.'

I nodded because I couldn't wait. We strolled around the park for a while, mixing with people, children and dogs of all shapes and sizes. Meanwhile, I tried my best to concentrate on being good and not getting distracted. A short while later, we'd left the park and were walking near some shops when I spotted something familiar – a black Labrador guide dog, who looked just like me!

'Hello,' I said, brightening up. It was like looking in a mirror because we were so alike. 'My name's Dez, what's yours?'

But the guide dog didn't move or speak. Instead, he sat still, staring straight ahead. Thinking he'd not heard me, I tried again.

'I'm a guide dog in training, but one day, I hope I'll become a proper guide dog, just like you.'

Silence. The dog refused to talk or even look at me. I felt offended.

'I'm sorry, I didn't mean to interrupt when you were working,' I stammered.

More silence followed.

Suddenly I heard a peel of laughter from behind – it was Niki.

'Oh, Dez,' she giggled, 'he's not a real dog!' She stepped

forward and tapped the 'dog' on the top of his head. A hollow sound rang out as she did so. 'It's a model - a fundraising dog model - to raise awareness of the Guide Dog charity.'

I blushed and nudged the plastic figure with my nose. She was right: he was rock solid. It was a dummy alright, but just then, I felt the biggest dummy of all!

'Come on,' Niki chuckled, 'let's try somewhere else.'

Part of being a good guide dog is getting used to different places and sounds, so that nothing scares you in the future. I thought back to the supermarket where I'd wet my pants and I felt my face flush bright red. I never, ever wanted that to happen again so I needed to experience absolutely everything if I wanted to be prepared. Niki decided we should walk down the high street, which was full of shops. Cars, vans and buses roared past me on the busy road, but I wasn't worried because by now, I was getting used to traffic. We continued to walk down the road when someone stopped her to ask directions to the library.

'I'm sorry,' she began to apologise, 'I'm not from round here. I was just...'

But her voice blurred against the wall of background noise because I'd spotted something – a giant strawberry cream cake sitting in the middle of the baker's shop window.

Hmmmm... my mouth drooled. *Luvvvverrrllllyyyy!*

There was a bit of slack on my lead and Niki was distracted, so I was able to inch a little closer. I pressed my nose against the shop window and tried to sniff the cake through solid glass.

It was definitely a strawberry cake, I decided. I could smell it, not through the glass, but through the open shop door. My mouth drooled and my belly rumbled – it smelt delicious!

Food. Cake. Strawberries. The words whirred through my mind as I lifted up my front paws and leaned against the shop front to get a better look.

Hmm... strawberries!

'Dez! What on earth...?'

It was Niki. I pulled my paws away sharply from underneath the window, but they felt tacky and wet. There was something on my paws but as I tried to look at them, I lost my balance and fell against the wall.

'*No!* It's just been painted. Look!' Niki gasped.

I looked over. Sure enough, there was a warning sign stuck to the wall, which read: WET PAINT – DO NOT TOUCH!

I panicked as I looked at both paws, covered in wet, white paint. The white gloss stood out like a sore thumb against my shiny black fur.

Sorry, Niki, I whined, begging for forgiveness.

But Niki wasn't cross; she was worried how she'd get the wet paint off me. Back home, we tried lots of different things. I even took a long soak in a paddling pool full of bubbles. Niki managed to get most of it off, but there were still a few stubborn bits on the front of my left paw.

'Hey, what's with the white paws?' Stan sniggered as soon as he saw me. He was talking to Marvellous Meg. Max was doing his usual – running around in great big circles.

'*Don't!*' I sighed, shaking my head with embarrassment.

'Why, what happened?' asked Meg.

So I told them about the cake in the window and the wet paint.

'Ha! So the strawberry thief has finally been caught, red-handed!' Stan chortled.

'Or rather white-pawed,' Meg added wryly.

Of course, it wasn't long before everyone had heard about the paint and me.

'I wouldn't worry about it,' said Meg as the others teased. 'The other day, I was in the woods, walking with Max, when he spotted a squirrel. He chased it but the squirrel was faster than him and shot straight up the tree.'

'What did he do?'

Meg raised a paw to her mouth to try and stifle her

giggles. 'That was it, you see: Max was running so fast that he bumped straight into the tree, head first! When he came round, he looked right and left, and asked, "Where did it go, where did it go..."'

I began to howl with laughter. 'He *didn't?*'

'He *did,*' Meg said, doubling up. 'He's a daft little thing, but he doesn't half make me laugh.'

Max's clumsiness certainly made me feel a little better about my own. I knew I had to learn how to control it, and also my greed, because pretty soon it would be time to leave and go to big school.

CHAPTER 10

MY BIRTHDAY
AND LEAVING PARTY

'Surprise!'

The room was packed with all my friends and family waiting for me. In the centre of the dining table was a huge birthday cake, made especially for dogs. It had my name and a huge number one written on the front in special doggy icing. Niki had even stuck a candle on top, which she lit and told me to blow out. I puffed up both cheeks, filling them full of air, and gave it a big blow. The flame flickered, swayed to one side, and then went out.

'Make a wish!' Niki called.

She was standing behind me with the rest of my family, who cheered and clapped along.

So I made my birthday wish – *to be the best guide dog in the world and make everyone proud of me* – but I didn't tell anyone because I wanted it to come true.

'I want to sing "Happy Birthday" to him!' Kilty barked, pushing through the crowd like a diva.

Stan groaned, dipped his head, and flattened the tips of his ears.

'As if we've not suffered enough,' Bonnie complained to Max, who for some reason was dressed in a stiff white formal shirt, complete with a bright purple dickie bow.

Meg noticed me looking over. 'He wanted to look smart for you,' she whispered. 'But you know Max, he always gets it wrong. When I said it was a party, he got all dressed up. I had to stop him from wearing his dinner jacket.'

Max grinned proudly, his shirt collar biting against his brown furry neck.

'Nice shirt,' I remarked, pointing to it.

'Oh, thanks! I bought it especially. I wanted to look smart, what with it being a special occasion and all.'

An awful shrill sound filled the room: Kilty had begun.

'Yappy birthday to you, Yappy birthday to yoooouuu, Yappy birthday, little Dezzy Boy, Yappy birthday to yoooooouuuuuuu!' her voice screeched, as everyone willed it to end.

When it did, we all clapped and cheered loudly, but only because it was over.

'Thanks, Kilty.' I blushed. 'Hey, I like your new collar!'

Kilty flushed a little and clasped a tiny white paw to her neck. She patted the diamanté collar fondly.

'It's from an admirer. I don't know who, but me money's on Harry Styles. I'm certain it's from him.'

I tried not to smirk. Her new necklace wasn't from Harry, because it was from me – it was a leaving present. Only when I'd handed it to Bonnie, I'd sworn her to secrecy. Just then, the doorbell rang and everyone started to bark wildly.

'Who is it? Perhaps it's another guest?' Max panted, excitedly.

'I'll get it,' Niki grinned as she headed for the front door.

Seconds later, we heard voices in the hallway. We waited, our ears straining, listening out for who it could be. Just then, the living room door swung open dramatically, brushing against the carpet. A solitary figure paused, standing there with a sour look on his face: it was Roger.

'*Don't!*' he said, holding up a paw as he swept into the room. 'I know what you're all thinking, but don't say a word!'

Everyone stopped to look at Roger, who was wearing...

No, surely not, it couldn't be... could it?

'Er, Roger,' Stan said, clearing his throat and breaking the awkward silence. 'Why are you wearing a pink tutu?'

Roger sighed, rolled his eyes and flopped miserably to the ground. 'That's why I'm late. Sorry, Dez,' he said, turning to me to apologise.

'It's okay,' I insisted.

Although I tried my best not to stare, I couldn't take my eyes off his sparkly tutu, though.

'It's her, isn't it?' Roger moaned, pointing a disgruntled

nose towards Mavis, who was talking away to Niki in the doorway. She was blissfully unaware of her pet's obvious discomfort. 'She said if I was going to a party then I had to wear a party dress, and this,' he said, fluffing up the skirt between both paws, 'is what she made me wear.'

'Er, and is that nail varnish I can spot with me old mince pies?' Winston piped up from the back of the room.

'Mince pies?' Roger asked, a little puzzled.

'Eyes!' we all chorused.

The Yorkshire terrier nodded his head, held out a paw and studied it glumly.

'It is. But I managed to stop her from putting two pairs of pink ballet pumps on my paws at t'last minute.'

'Poor Roger,' Max sympathised. He lifted up his front paw and loosened the oversized dickie bow from around his neck.

Roger sighed wearily. 'Aye, when she tried to do that, I reckoned t'nail varnish were least of me worries.'

The room fell silent as his eyes darted around, waiting for someone to laugh or poke fun, but no one did because we all felt sorry for him. Roger was our friend and right now he was upset. He lifted his sad little face and stared at Winston.

'Nice shirt, by the way.'

The bulldog stood up proudly, back as straight as an iron rod as though he was on parade. 'It's made from a Union Jack flag,' he barked as he patted a paw against his heart. 'I'm proud to be British, and proud to be a bulldog.'

Roger nodded and turned. As he did so, he spied the cake in the middle of the table.

'Oh, I didn't miss t'candle being blown out on t'cake, did I?'

'You did, but don't worry, I'll get Niki to cut it up and then we can all have a slice,' I reassured him.

'Just a slither for me,' Kilty called. 'I'm watching me figure, pet.'

'Not too much for me, either,' Willow added, batting her eyelashes in Stan's direction, '...because someone's taking me out for dinner.'

'Whooooooo!' we all chorused.

Stan blushed as Niki appeared with some paper plates. She cut up the cake and handed everyone a slice. Soon we were all tucking into bowls of water and plates of home-baked doggy birthday cake.

'NOM, NOM, NOM!'

'Shame it's not strawberry-flavoured, eh?' said Stan, giving me a nudge.

'*Don't!*' I grunted, in between mouthfuls.

'I see you've still got the one white paw then.'

'I know!' I muttered, lifting it up. 'Talk about standing out from the crowd.'

'So,' said Stan, hoovering up the last crumbs of cake. 'When do you go to big school?'

'Monday, although I have to say, I'm a bit frightened.'

'Why?'

'What if I'm rubbish, Stan? What if I get everything wrong or say the wrong thing? What then?'

'But you won't. You'll be great, because it's what you were born to do.'

I shook my head. 'And then there's Niki, Jon and the children, I'm gonna miss them like mad!' I mumbled, my voice quivering as my eyes brimmed with tears.

Stan lifted his head out of his water bowl and straightened up.

'Look, son. You were frightened when you first arrived here, and look how many friends you've made. Everyone loves you!'

I glanced around the room. Stan was right – it was packed with all my doggy pals. Kilty was at the back, holding Roger's tutu down with two paws as he tried to wriggle out of it.

'And you're sure I can have it, if we get it off in one piece?' she was asking.

'You can burn it, for all I care,' Roger moaned.

Winston was in a corner, chatting to Meg and Max,

while Willow was standing next to Bonnie, who was already munching through her second slice of cake.

The whole gang was there.

'Okay, you're right. It's just... well, I just don't want to make a fool of myself, that's all, because being a guide dog is all I've ever wanted to be.'

'And you will be great,' Stan insisted, patting me on the back. 'Although right now, you've got a great big crumb on the side of your mouth.'

I stuck out my tongue to try and lick it off, but there was nothing there.

'No, the other side,' said Stan, pointing.

Within a nanosecond it had gone.

'Come on, cheer up, Dez!' he coaxed, wrapping a paw around my shoulder. 'Besides, I thought this was meant to be a party.'

'Er, it is.'

'In that case, we need some MUSIC!'

'Ooh, can we have some Snoop Dogg?' Max panted, as he raced over. 'I love a bit of gangster rap!'

'Nah,' Winston barked. 'Let's have "Who let the dogs out... who hoo hoo hoo hoo..."'

Everyone howled until the whole room was in an uproar. Niki walked over to the side and plugged the iPod into a speaker dock. The sound of 'Dog Days Are Over' by Florence and the Machine filled the room.

'Oh, I love this one! Wanna dance, pet?' Kilty said, bouncing over and grabbing me by the paw before I could say no.

Stan winked at me.

'I'd love to.' I blushed.

We danced all afternoon and played lots of party games, but all too soon it was time to say goodbye.

'So, I guess this is it then, guys. I'm off to big school on Monday,' I sighed sadly, shrugging my shoulders.

'You take care of yourself,' said Marvellous Meg, stepping forward to give me a hug first. 'And don't forget to call.'

'See you then, mate!' Max said, punching me a little too hard on the shoulder. 'Oops, sorry! I don't wanna damage you before you get there, eh?' he chuckled, before spinning around in circles.

Just watching him was enough to make me feel dizzy.

'Bye then,' Meg waved, pulling Max by the shirt collar.

'Woof!' he barked excitedly, and then they were gone.

'Take care, pet,' Bonnie sobbed, pulling me into a huge hug.

'And don't forget to text me,' Kilty insisted, pointing at her phone. She looked a little red-eyed, as though she'd been crying.

'Are you okay?' I asked.

'I'm fine, pet. I've just got summat in me eye,' she sniffed. She dipped forward to kiss me on the cheek. 'Now don't forget, will ya? You'd better text us!'

'I will,' I promised, trying to compose myself. 'And I'll look out for you on X *Factor*,' I said, crossing my front paws.

Kilty smiled as she and Bonnie headed for the door.

'Take care, bin lid,' a gruff voice boomed, making me turn sharply.

'Thanks, Winston.' I grinned.

'Come on, Rog, time we were off, eh?' he said, glancing down at his little mate.

'Hey, your tutu! What happened?' I asked.

Roger held up a paw against the side of his mouth and whispered to me secretly: 'Kilty and I, we ripped it, getting it off, so I flushed it down the toilet!' His gritted little teeth flashed as he whispered through them. 'But don't tell anyone, will you?'

I crossed my heart with my front paw. Just then, Mavis shouted.

'Rachel, Rachel, where's my little princess? Oh, there you are!' she beamed, scooping Roger up in both arms. He twisted his head to look back at us and rolled his eyes skywards.

'See you later then, lads. And good luck, Dez! Let us know how you get on, won't you?'

'I will, Rog,' I promised, waving as Winston followed him to the door.

Willow stepped forward in the now-empty room and gave me a quick peck on the cheek.

'Good luck, Dez. We're all rooting for you!' she said, swiping a paw in front of her.

She turned to face Stan and fluttered her eyelashes.

'...and I'll wait for you by the door, handsome.'

Soon, there was just Stan and me left, although somehow it felt awkward because neither of us knew what to say.

'Well, I guess this is it. Put it there,' he said, holding out a front paw for me to shake. 'I have to say, it's been a real pleasure – showing you the ropes, park life, and all.'

'And I've loved every single second of it!' I said, taking his paw firmly in mine. 'Thank you, Stan! Thank you for teaching me how to become a proper dog. If I grow up to be a patch on you, then I'll be happy.'

Stan shrugged. 'Shucks, I dunno what to say, but you'll be great! Now, get yourself off to that Guide Dog School and show them how it's done.'

'I will, Stan, and I'll make you proud of me, I promise.'

CHAPTER 11

BIG SCHOOL

'I don't think I can watch,' Niki sobbed, as she kissed me goodbye at the front door.

I was standing there, waiting for the car to arrive to take me to big school, the suitcase on the floor by my side.

'I've packed your teddy and your blankie,' Niki said, trying to put on a brave face, but I knew how upset she was. She was rubbish at hiding how much she loved me and I was the same.

I'll miss you all, I choked, wiping a solitary tear from my eye before anyone noticed.

Suddenly, there was the sound of a car horn beeping outside: it was time.

'I love you, Dez,' Niki wept, giving me a cuddle.

I nuzzled against the side of her neck and licked her face.

Love you too, Niki. What am I going to do without you, Jon, Sam, Harry and Molly? I fretted.

Soon it was time as, one by one, I said goodbye to my puppy-walker family. To be honest, although I was excited about going to big school, I didn't want to leave. I knew Guide Dogs would write to Niki to let her know how I was getting on, but I also knew how much I was going to miss her, the rest of my family and my gang of mates. I waved out of the window after I climbed into the back of the car. As it wound its way along the street, I held my head high and tried to be brave as I watched my family disappear off into the distance. My stomach clenched with anxiety.

What if I mess up again? What if I don't make any new friends?

I felt scared because I didn't know what to expect or just how difficult it would be. All these worries swam around inside my head as the car trundled along the road. We'd been driving for around forty-five minutes when the driver indicated, slowed and turned into a car park. I was clipped onto a lead and taken inside. Although I tried to act grown-up and brave, inside my belly was rumbling with nerves. Once I'd been checked in, I was taken to the National Guide Dog School, which housed dozens of other young, but almost adult, pups about to start training.

'Ah, I see we have a new recruit,' a voice barked as soon as I entered the room.

I glanced up to see a German Shepherd dog.

'Now then, solider,' he barked, prodding me sharply with a cane. 'You are here to learn. This will be your kennel, which you will sleep in, but keep it clean at all times. Do I make myself clear?'

'Yyy... yes, sir!' I woofed, standing to attention.

'Good, good! That's what I like to see, a young dog who knows his place.'

I felt my knees wobble.

'Now, get yourself unpacked and report for duty at 12.00 hours at the front of the kennels. I need you over there. See?' he said, pointing towards the front of the room.

I took a huge gulp and nodded to indicate that I'd understood.

Blimey, I didn't think Guide Dog School would be this strict...

'Righto! Well, we have rules here, young man. Rules which must not be broken...' he said, striding up and down in front of me, barking orders.

Suddenly a voice interrupted him in full flow.

'Oh, Major, that's where you've got to! I was looking all

over for you,' a woman sighed, clipping on his lead. 'Now,' she said, straightening up. 'I hope you haven't been bossing the little ones around.'

'B–but, this is preposterous,' he snorted angrily. 'I was just telling this new recruit...'

'Come on, Major. It's time for a walk,' she said, leading him away.

My body relaxed as the breath I'd been holding came rushing out.

'Ignore him, Dez. He likes to think he's in charge.'

The voice sounded so familiar it made me turn in my tracks.

'Vesper!' I gasped.

'Alright, bro?' he grinned, fist-bumping my paw. 'We wondered what time you'd get here.'

'Why?' I asked. 'Who else is here?'

'Vinnie, Vicky, all the family... Everyone apart from Vi.'

'Violet, oh, I know.' I nodded. 'She texted me to tell me what had happened.'

Vesper shrugged. 'Yep, it's a shame but Mum says Violet's doing really well as a buddy dog. She's changed, our Violet, she's finally grown up.'

'You mean she's nice now.'

A voice called from behind him: it was Vicky. She was standing with Vinnie. I ran towards them both to give them a hug.

'It's great to see you,' Vicky said, her eyes filling with tears. 'I've really missed you.'

'Me too,' I admitted.

'Not too close,' Vinnie said, holding up a paw to halt me. 'I've not been well and...'

'Oh, Vinnie!' I laughed, pulling him close. 'You never change.'

'But *you* do,' Vinnie sniffed. 'You look, well, you suddenly look all grown-up.'

'I guess we all do,' Vicky agreed, as we looked each other up and down.

We talked long into the afternoon as the others warned me what to expect.

'There's lots of walking – and fun! But you have to train hard. You have to pass all your exams if you want to become a guide dog,' Vesper explained.

'Just because you came top of your class,' Vicky teased.

'Naturally,' Vesper said, polishing his nails against the fur of his chest, 'and so will all of you, because we're related, so it's in the family!'

The following day, I began my training. I was taught how to follow simple commands. Niki had already taught me the basics – how to eat my food on the blow of the whistle, how the words 'busy, busy' meant to go for a wee, but now I had to learn how to walk in a straight line and with no pulling on the lead. I found that especially hard because I was always in such a rush to get to the next place. Then I was taught my left from right, which, unlike the others, I found easy, thanks to my white left paw. I was given my very own personal trainer to work with, who was lovely. There were six of us in total taught by the same woman. Once I'd got to know her, she introduced me to the metal harness, which I'd be expected to wear once I became a guide dog. Unlike others in my group, I didn't flinch when she first put it over my head. I didn't flinch because I knew I'd get a treat.

'Well done, Dez!' she said, handing me my treat, patting me lovingly.

That night, I thought I'd text Stan to let him know how things were going.

'*Itz great here,*' I typed. '*I've met up with my family and I'm learning lotz of new thingz. Give my love to the rest of the gang, Dez x*'

Stan replied almost immediately. '*Hi Dez, we all wondered how you were getting on. It's great to hear from you. Glad you're enjoying it there. Take care of yourself, S x*
Ps: Why do you keep spelling things wrong with a Z instead of an S? Don't they teach you spelling at Guide Dog School, eh? Lol x'

'Oops!' I giggled (I'd never been good at spelling).

Each night that followed, while the others sat around chatting or watching TV, I'd sit in my kennel, swotting up on everything we'd learned, because I was determined to become the best guide dog the school had ever seen.

'Well done, Valdez, you're going to make a great guide dog!' the teacher said one day, after class. She patted me fondly on the top of my head and I was so thrilled, I thought I'd burst.

'Congratulations, little bruv,' Vicky whispered proudly.

It felt good because all my hard work was slowly starting to pay off. Finally, I'd learned to control my hunger because

I'd stopped letting my belly rule my head. Instead I worked hard until soon I'd become top of every class!

'Is this where the teacher's pet lives?' a voice called as a paw knocked against the wall of my pen.

My nose was in a book but I glanced up to see a familiar golden head dip around the corner.

'Star!' I cried, dropping the book and running towards her.

'Hello, Dez. I was in the area, so I thought I'd just drop by...'

But she didn't finish her sentence because I was kissing and squeezing the life out of her.

'It's so good to see you, I've really missed you!' I sighed, holding her close.

'Me too! Now, everyone tells me that what you don't know about guide dog training isn't worth knowing, so I'm hoping you'll help me.'

'Of course I will. Now, come here,' I said, patting a cushion on the floor. 'Take a seat.'

I told Star all about left and right, the walking in a straight line, and trying not to pull on the lead. 'That's the tricky bit,' I sighed, 'knowing when to slow down and when to speed up. You have to see how fast they're walking and take your lead from them.'

Star shook her head, saying, 'It's hopeless. I'm never gonna remember all of this, Dez.'

'You will. It just takes lots of practice, that's all.'

The months passed and soon I was walking along wearing the harness without complaint. Then it was time to learn how to guess distances. The trainer would walk me by an object, such as a chair, but then she'd stop and tap it. At first I thought she'd gone completely mad because she started tapping the top of doors, the side of chairs, even the edges of lamp posts. I was baffled until something clicked inside my brain: I realised she wanted me to be able to judge how far or how close things were. I needed to know if I could get through a space with someone at my side, because once I had an owner, I'd have to be their eyes. We practised again and again, until I knew it off by heart. I was so good that I knew exactly what to look out for and how to react.

Despite coming top of my class, my walking speed was a real problem. I was a fast walker, and I knew Guide Dogs would have to match me with someone who walked quickly so I could keep up with them (and them with me). Soon, I was ready for my final exam – the blindfold walk. I was shaking like a jellybean because it was my big moment and I didn't want to mess up so I tried to remember everything I'd learned in class. I remembered the main thing was to keep calm and think about every single thing I did, because if I put just one paw wrong, it'd all be over. My mouth felt dry, and my stomach churned like a washing machine as my trainer led me towards the busy main street.

Keep calm, Dez. Keep calm, I repeated over and over to myself inside my head, but my legs were trembling and my paws were sweating.

'Come on, Dez, I know you can do it!' the trainer encouraged me.

I knew I'd have someone watching me, giving me marks, and I felt really nervous. My trainer was blindfolded as we walked along. Traffic whizzed by; it made me gasp because it was both noisy and smelly. I tried my best to concentrate because I knew if I messed this up then I'd never become a guide dog. We walked for ages, but now I knew how to do things safely. If anything, I was so safe that they called me the 'road safety dog' because I always watched, waited and listened before crossing. I'd find somewhere safe to cross but I'd stop before we reached the kerb. Then I'd take my time, sit down and look out for traffic. When it was coming, I'd let it pass because I knew it wasn't worth taking the risk and, when it was safe, I'd cross but I never ran because I had to be in control at all times.

'Well done, Dez!' the trainer said as we reached the end of the test. She pulled off her blindfold, bent down and gave me a lovely ear rub. 'You were a complete star!'

So, have I passed, then? I asked, looking up at her.

'Top of the class!' she grinned, patting me fondly on my back.

Whoopee! My tail began to wag and it wouldn't stop. I'd passed and now I was officially a guide dog – I could barely believe it.

'I passed today!' I squealed later down the phone to Mum.

'Oh, Dez, I knew you would!' she cried. 'I told you that you were my special boy. You'll be top of the list now, just you wait and see, because everyone will want you!'

CHAPTER 12

LAST ON
THE SHELF

I waited and waited for someone to come and take me to my new home. Every time one of the mobility instructors walked in, my heart would lift, but they always chose another dog instead of me. It was the instructor's job to match each dog to each person but it seemed there wasn't a match for me.

'What's wrong with me, Star?' I cried, one night after dinner. 'Why doesn't anyone want me?'

Star shook her head.

'I dunno, Dez. I don't understand it. I mean, you came top of your class.'

But it didn't seem to count as, one by one, I watched as Vicky, Vinnie and Vesper left me behind. Soon, it was time for Star to go too.

'I know someone will want you. You'll be chosen soon, I promise,' she said, giving me a final hug goodbye.

I willed my tears to go away because I wanted to believe

her – that there was someone out there, waiting for me – but the more I wished for it to happen, the more disappointed I felt when it didn't. Soon, everyone had been given a new home – everyone apart from me. To make matters worse, a new intake of dogs had arrived.

'See him over there,' one pup whispered to another, 'no one wants him. He's clever too – it's just he's a really fast walker, so they can't find anyone to match him with.'

The other one glanced over.

'It's so sad,' she sighed.

That made me feel even worse. Soon, I felt so sad that I could barely bring myself to eat.

So much for my big dreams, I huffed as I lay on the floor, trying to work out where it had all gone wrong. The following day, I was still feeling sorry for myself when the door swung open as the trainer showed someone inside. My head bobbed up hopefully, but then I heard her speak.

'Gwyn is just through here,' she said.

I sighed and let my head drop back down sadly on my paws. Both women were just walking past my kennel when the mobility instructor stopped and looked at me.

'What about this one, with the white left paw?' she asked, holding out her hand to stroke me.

I was so delighted to be noticed that I stood up and started wagging my tail wildly.

'This is Valdez, or Dez. He's a beautiful boy, he's just a little fast and erm... over-enthusiastic,' the trainer explained.

'Is he now?' the woman replied. 'Well, I recognise this one. I saw his picture on the Guide Dogs webpage, and I think I may know just the person for him.'

She grinned as I realised just what it was she was saying.

Pick me, pick me! I woofed. *You won't regret it, I promise. I'll try my very best. I won't let you down. Please pick me!* My tail wagged so much it made my whole body swing from side to side. Soon I was having trouble staying on all four paws.

'Hello, Dez. My name is Emma,' she said kindly, dipping down to give me a lovely ear rub. 'I think I know just the person for you.'

I liked Emma immediately. She had such a kind and

133

gentle face that I desperately wanted to try my best for her.

'I'd love to take them both – Valdez and Gwyn, if that's okay?' she asked.

Yessssss! I whooped, my paw punching the air with delight. *A new home and a new start!* I could barely contain my excitement.

Emma went off to collect the other dog, a German Shepherd called Gwyn, and we were both put in the back of her car.

'Excuse me,' Gwyn said in a posh voice. 'Do you mind? You appear to be standing on my foot.'

'Oops!' I giggled, trying to look out of the window. 'Sorry,' I panted. 'It's just I'm so very excited. You see, I've waited for this for such a long time…'

'Err, yes,' Lady Gwyn sniffed, looking down her nose at me. 'I can tell. Now, if you don't mind, I'd like to rest during the journey because I like to feel refreshed when we arrive at our destination, so a little peace and quiet would be rather nice.'

Gwyn folded her legs elegantly beneath her like a ballet dancer and curled up on the floor. She rested her pretty little face on her paws and closed her eyes.

'So, how long have you been waiting? I mean, are you excited about going to your new home? What do you think it'll be like? Do you think—'

Gwyn raised a paw to stop me.

'When I said "rest", I meant no talking. Now then, paws on lips,' she said, holding a paw haughtily up to her mouth.

'But I... b–buu...'

'Shush!' Gwyn snapped. 'I SAID paws on lips!'

Her voice was so shrill that I immediately clamped a paw over my mouth.

'Thank you,' she sighed. 'Now, if you could stay like that for the whole journey, then I'd be most grateful.'

Gwyn settled down once more and closed her eyes. Moments later, she opened one and looked directly at me.

'By the way, I didn't say for you to stop breathing.'

I let out the breath I'd been holding inside as it came rushing out.

GASP!

'Thank goodness for that!' I panted.

Lady Gwyn tutted and turned away disapprovingly.

'Honestly, working-class Labradors! Where on earth do they get you from, hmm?' she muttered, before settling down to sleep.

Soon, the car had pulled up outside a house and Lady Gwyn stepped down onto the pavement.

'See you again soon, I hope,' I said, grinning like a lunatic.

Gwyn turned back to look at me. 'Yes, yes, I suppose... if I *must*!'

A short while later, we'd pulled up outside another house and Emma opened the car door.

'This is Yvonne's house. She will be your boarder, until you're ready to go to live at your new home,' she explained, leading me to the front door.

Yvonne was lovely and gave me lots of love and cuddles. As Emma left, I wandered over to the window to watch her go, but then she did something quite unexpected. Instead of driving away, she locked the car and walked into the garden of a house only a few doors away. I glanced up at Yvonne, a little puzzled.

'Yes, Dez, that's right,' Yvonne said, rubbing the side of my face. 'Emma is our neighbour.'

CHAPTER 13

THE SURPRISE

'Oh no, not you again!' Lady Gwyn sniffed as she hopped daintily into the back of the car. 'I thought I'd be mixing with a better breed of dog.'

She sniffed, holding a white, lacy handkerchief up against her nose as though she might catch something.

'Hello, Gwyn,' I said, slumping down on my bum so that I could scratch an itch near my collar with my back paw.

'Urgh! I *do* hope you haven't got fleas!' Lady Gwyn screeched, backing away from me.

'Nope,' I said, a daft grin sweeping across on my face. 'Just an itch that needs to be scratched, you know.'

I knew it wasn't funny but I couldn't stop smiling because I was just so happy to be there.

The car started up and fired into life as Emma drove along the road.

'So,' I said, trying to make conversation, 'I wonder what our new owners will be like.'

'I already know who mine is,' Gwyn replied, fixing me with a withering stare. 'Why? Don't you know who your owner will be?'

'Nope,' I said, shaking my head. 'But it all adds to the fun, I suppose, doesn't it?'

I stared ahead as Emma indicated and pulled the car over, parking up by the side of some trees.

'Looks like a park, looks like a park!' I woofed excitedly, as I danced around in the back of the car.

'Oh, for goodness sake!' Lady Gwyn snapped. 'I do hope you can control yourself, because I don't think I can stand four months of this. It's like, I don't know, it's like living with a toddler pup or something!'

Just then, Emma opened up the back door.

'Right, who's first then?' she said, looking down at us both.

Pick me, pick me! I panted, holding my paw up in the air. *Please, miss, please pick me!*

'Oh, for goodness sake! Go on, *go!* Hurry up and get it over with,' Lady Gwyn huffed, lying down again. 'Then at least I'll be able to have a bit of peace and quiet.'

'Well, it looks like you're first, Dez!' Emma decided. 'Come on, then!'

That day, I practised walking on the lead and the harness. I knew I'd have to do another walking exam with my new owner, so I needed to practise so I'd be ready for it. I tried my best to concentrate because I wanted to show Emma just how good I could be.

'You're doing great, Dez,' she said, encouraging me. 'I just need you to slow down a bit because you always give 110 per cent!'

Sorry, Emma, I barked, looking up at her with big brown eyes.

The next few times we went out, I tried my best to calm down.

Slow, slow, slow... I said, trying to tell my paws to move a little slower.

'Better,' Emma said, beaming down at me.

I was so thrilled that I wagged my tail furiously in the air. Finally, I was starting to get the hang of it! After three months, I was beginning to feel ready for my new home and owner, even though I was dreading my last and final guide-dog walking exam. I thought about my new owner.

What will he or she be like? I wondered.

That morning, when Emma came to pick me up, she told me that Lady Gwyn had already left for her new home. My stomach knotted inside.

I hope I'm not last on the shelf again... I fretted.

But I needn't have worried, because Emma had a plan. She sat down beside me and began to explain.

'Right, Dez! Today, you're going to meet someone very special. His name is John Tovey and he needs a guide dog. I think you'll like him, Dez, because John's a worrier, like you.' She smiled and paused for a moment before continuing. 'Anyway, the plan is, I need you to walk with him, but because he's blind, he won't know it's you. Do you understand?'

I nodded my head to show that I did.

'Right, John has already been out walking with a few practise dogs, so he'll think you're one of them.'

Okaaay, I thought, sitting down for a moment. I'd wondered where this was leading.

'He'll actually be walking with you, but I don't want him to know it's you otherwise he'll be a bundle of nerves. He's just like you, and I can't have you both a bundle of nerves, so you see, Dez, it's a surprise – and it'll only be a secret until the walk is over. That's when I'll tell John it's you. So you mustn't say anything or let the cat out of the bag, do you understand?'

Cat? I sprang up onto all fours and glanced around.

Cats? Cats? Nobody said anything about cats!

'I mean,' said Emma, realising my confusion, 'you mustn't tell John it's you – well, not until after the walk. That way, I'll know if you two are meant to be together.'

Ah, right! Now I get it.

Emma put me in the car and we drove to a flat in a little village on the outskirts of Bristol. I watched nervously as a tall, slim man with dark hair climbed in and sat in the passenger seat next to her. My ears strained as he started to talk in the front of the car.

He sounds really nice, I thought, excitement rising inside me. *Calm down, Dez*, I told myself, as I took a deep breath. *Remember what Emma said: don't get too giddy because this is important. This is your big chance – you mustn't blow it!*

When Emma opened the car door, I didn't rush out; instead I sat and waited until she told me it was okay to jump down. Then I stood as still as a statue while she looped my head through the metal harness. I tried to remember everything I'd been taught at Guide Dog School.

Keep calm and think about what you're doing. And whatever you do, don't walk too FAST!

John took the brace as I waited for the command. I could feel his hand trembling on the harness. Emma was right, he was as nervous as I was.

'Right, I'd like you to walk with Volley,' Emma said, her voice loud and clear.

I winked at her to let her know I understood. For the next half-hour I would pretend to be Volley, whoever he was. Emma looked down to check I was ready – I was. John called out and asked me to go 'forward'. I recognised this immediately, it was a guide dog command for walk. I put one paw in front of the other and began to move along slowly. Soon, we were walking along pavements and stopping at roadsides, as Emma watched and observed. I looked up to try and guess how I was doing, but she was so busy watching, I couldn't tell. The walk went so well that I felt as though I'd been with John for years, not minutes. When we finally came to a halt, a wide grin spread across Emma's face.

'John,' she said.

'Hmm?' John replied, lifting his head slightly.

'You know I said I had a dog for you?'

'Hmm,' he said, patting me on the head.

'Well, this is him. This is a dog called Dez.'

I looked up at John, worried he'd be cross with me for

tricking him because I'd pretended to be Volley, but instead
he crouched down onto his knees and gave me a massive
cuddle. Gratefully, I kissed the back of his hand.

'Is he mine? I mean, is he *really* mine, all mine, to keep?'
he asked.

I held my breath as we both waited for the answer.

'He is.' Emma smiled.

'*Yesssss!*' said John, punching the air. He cried with joy
as I kicked up my paws and did a celebration dance in the
middle of the pavement.

At last, I was a proper guide dog, with a proper owner!
Now, I finally belonged.

CHAPTER 14

FIRST STEPS

It was my big day, the day I left to go and live at John's house. So I took out my mobile and texted Stan.

Hi Stan, it's me. Guess what? I'm now a proper guide dog with an owner and everything. His name is John, and he's great! Just one more walking exam to go (which I'm dreading), then I'm fully qualified. Tell the gang I miss them, Dez x

Stan replied almost immediately.

That's great news! Just wait until I tell everyone, they'll be so proud. Good luck in your new job and with your new life. Don't forget to keep in touch, and don't go nicking any more strawberries because you're almost a guide dog! Lol, S x

Just then Emma knocked at Yvonne's door: it was time to leave. I felt sad when I kissed Yvonne goodbye and jumped into the back of the car, because I'd loved living with her. A short while later, we pulled up outside John's house. Emma clipped on my lead and we walked to the front door.

She pressed the intercom doorbell as we waited. It crackled slightly as someone picked it up.

'Hi John, it's Emma. I've got someone here who's really excited to meet you again!'

'It's Dez,' I woofed, barely able to contain my excitement. But I whimpered as a horrible thought gripped me. *What if he didn't remember me? What if John, my new dad, had changed his mind?* My stomach clenched with fear because I so wanted to come and live with him.

I heard a muffled noise as he undid the lock on the door.

Hi John! I cried, as soon as I saw him. *Is this your home, can I look around, can I? Is this where we're gonna live? Is this my new home?* I panted, scrambling from room to room to have a good nosey around.

'*Blimey!*' John grinned, as I whizzed past him. 'He's like a whirlwind!'

I pushed open the door to the front room and that's when I saw it – a huge pile of dog toys, all for me!

Are these for me, all for me? I gasped, my tail whirring high in the air like a mini helicopter. I ran over and grabbed the first toy I could see. As I did so, a squeak pierced the air.

It squeaks! Did you hear that? I said, dropping the toy and running back to tell him, even though I knew he couldn't hear or understand my dog speak. *It squeaks! Whooaaa... I'm gonna go back in there and find it again!* I grabbed the toy and when it squeaked a second time, I almost wet myself with excitement. *This was great!*

'I hope you're going to be happy here, Dez,' John said, as

I settled down on the floor at his side. 'And I hope you'll call me Dad, because I think I'd like that.'

You betcha! I barked happily.

I lifted up my nose and sniffed the air.

Kitchen!

I bounded into it and spied a box of food on top of the work surface.

'Has he found his food?' Dad asked Emma, outside in the corridor. She bobbed her head around the kitchen door to look at me.

'Nope, but I think he can definitely smell it.'

Food... food? I begged hopefully. But Dad refused because it wasn't dinner-time, not just yet, anyway.

Emma sat down and had a cup of tea. She told Dad that as a guide dog owner, he must follow certain rules.

'Remember, no dogs on furniture and don't go out, not just yet. You can let him out for a wee in the back garden, but that's it. Just spend the weekend chilling out, getting to know one another.'

Oh, we will! I thought happily.

'Right,' said Emma, finally getting to her feet. 'I guess we're all done here. I'll see you on Monday, John and Dez,' she grinned, bending down to give me a good ear rub.

Right a bit, down. Nope. Left a bit, now up... Ooh, there you go – spot on! I sighed, nuzzling against the side of her hand.

After Emma had left, I picked up a piece of rope and tried to get my new dad involved in a game of tug of war. I won, of course. After a while, I needed a wee, but I forgot Dad couldn't see when I went over to the patio door so I whimpered and tapped my paw so he could hear me. He opened it, but then he stood there, waiting for me to come back in.

'Good boy!' he praised as I ran through the door.

Blimey, Dad, it was only a wee! I blushed.

As soon as he sat down on the sofa, I went over and nestled down on the ground beside his feet. After a few hours, my eyes started to feel heavy so I wandered over to my new bed, which was soft, warm and very, very comfortable. I was just nodding off when Dad came over and laid beside me, resting his hand against my side. I must have fallen asleep because when I finally opened my eyes it was dark and he'd gone to bed. I shut them again, but then I felt a hand against my heart, checking it was still beating.

Wake me up, why don't you? I thought grumpily as he continued to check on me throughout the night.

The following morning, I could hear him snoring in bed, so I decided to get my own back. It was dark outside and still early as I ran full pelt towards the door.

DOOF!

I kicked open his bedroom door with my front paws and dived straight on top of Dad and the bed.

'Whooaa!' He laughed, begging for mercy.

Come on then, get up, get up! I giggled, nuzzling my wet nose underneath his chin to hurry him.

'Hang on a minute, Dez! I just need to get dressed...'

But I couldn't wait. Grabbing a corner of the duvet between my teeth, I pulled and pulled until I'd completely dragged it off him.

Come on, lazy bones! I insisted.

Dad was shivering because he was only wearing a pair of boxer shorts, but I was determined he was getting up because I wanted to play, eat breakfast and have some fun! It took a bit of persuasion and lots of bullying on my part, but soon I'd got my wish. With my belly full, Dad grabbed a towel and headed over into the bathroom. There was no lock on the door, so I knew exactly what I had to do. As soon as I heard the jet of water splash in the bathtub and the shower curtain close, I slipped in, undetected. I lay there, curled up on the bathmat, trying not to kill myself laughing.

This will give you a shock! I giggled mischievously.

A few moments later, Dad twisted off the shower and stepped out onto the bathmat. But it was *me*, a furry bath-mat with a heartbeat!

'Dez!' he exclaimed, bursting out laughing.

Dad bent down to stroke the fur on the back of my head.

I didn't want to move because I wanted to be with him all the time. From now on, I would be his eyes and ears and I'd always be there to protect him. I'd be his best friend and his guide dog. But the more he stroked me, the sleepier I felt, until soon I was curled up fast asleep on the bathroom floor. I was such a big lump that, unable to see, Dad almost tripped over me.

Oops, sorry! I giggled.

That weekend, we had the most fabulous time together, even though we didn't leave the flat once. We weren't allowed to go out until we'd both passed our 'walking test', which I was dreading. It was to be my final test, but I felt just as nervous as I'd been before my very first exam in puppy school. Emma was due to call by in the morning so that we could start training all over again. I only hoped I wouldn't mess up or disappoint anyone.

Unlike before, this time I wouldn't be alone because it'd be Dad and me training together as a team. That's what we'd be from now on: John and Dez, or Dez and John, and together we'd take on the world!

CHAPTER 15

CAUGHT ON TV

'So you want me to throw it?' asked Dad.

I whimpered with delight.

Course I do! Throw it, throw it... throw the toy! I woofed.

I was so giddy and my tail was swinging so much that I thought I'd take off, like a Labrador helicopter.

'Okay, one, two, three...'

Dad's arm swung forward as the soft toy flew up through the air. I kept my eye on it the whole time as it sailed over my head.

PLOP!

It had landed in the middle of the garden, so I dashed over to retrieve it.

'This is fun.' Dad grinned. He took it from my mouth and threw it again.

Eh? What on earth is he doing? I wondered. Once was fun, but twice...?

I glanced back at Dad, who was waiting for me to bring it back again.

Go on, then, I muttered under my breath. *But if you throw it one more time, then you'll have to fetch it yourself.*

He took the toy from my mouth, and I watched in disbelief as he threw it a THIRD time.

Maybe he doesn't want it? Maybe he's trying to throw it away? I thought randomly, as I looked over at the toy on the ground.

Dad was standing there waiting.

What was he waiting for? If he wanted the toy, then why did he throw it away? It made no sense.

We stood there with me looking up at Dad and him saying nothing. I was just wondering what I should do when his voice broke the silence.

'Dez... Dez...!' he called out in a panic.

Don't panic! I'm right here, Dad, I whimpered, nuzzling against the palm of his hand.

'Oh, thank goodness, for a moment I thought...' His voice tailed off as he felt around my mouth.

Humphf! What are you doing? Gerroff! I huffed as his fingers felt my mouth.

Suddenly Dad dropped onto his hands and knees like a dog.

What on earth was he doing now? Had he gone mad?

I heard him muttering something about the toy – the toy he didn't want, the toy he'd thrown away.

What was going on?

I shook my head as Dad crawled up and down the garden, searching for something.

What is it, Dad? I whimpered. What have you lost? Can I help? Oh, let me help, please!

But I didn't know what it was he'd lost. Instead, I sat down and watched as he crawled along the grass, his hands outstretched, feeling for something.

What on earth? Hey, watch out! Mind the dog poo! I winced as Dad's hand narrowly missed a pile of my doggy doo.

What is it? Did you drop something? I can be a search dog, I can help you, I said. Only Dad didn't speak Labrador, so he didn't have a clue what I was saying.

'Ah, here it is!' he said, clutching the toy in his hand as though it were treasure. 'I thought it'd gone over the back fence or something, but it was here all the time, just where I'd thrown it.'

I looked at him.

Yes, Dad. It was there where you'd thrown it AWAY! If you wanted it back, then why didn't you say so? I knew he couldn't see, but all he'd had to do was ask.

Humans can be so confusing, I thought.

But then I worried. *What if Dad was angry? What if he wanted to send me back? I wasn't a very good guide dog if I hadn't realised all he'd wanted to do was bring the toy back!*

However, Dad started to laugh.

'Oh Dez,' he chuckled. 'You *are* funny!'

At this I scratched my head with my paw.

Funny? I didn't understand. I hadn't told a joke or anything, so what was funny?

151

As I sat there, trying to work out what he'd meant, I heard the intercom. I sprang to my feet – Emma had arrived.

Emma, Emma, Emma! I whimpered with delight. I was happy to see her.

'Hello Dez,' she said, bending down to give me a good ear rub.

Just there, just there! I murmured, turning my head lovingly towards her. *Yeah, you got it!*

It was time to start work, namely teaching John how to put my harness on properly. A guide-dog harness is a tricky thing to put on a dog, but it's even trickier when you're blind, so I knew it'd take a while. Dad huffed a bit, but eventually, after clonking me on the head a few times by accident, he got the hang of it.

Thank goodness for that! I sighed, rubbing my forehead with my paw.

'Well done, John,' Emma congratulated him. 'Now, I'd like you to do it again.'

Again? What? No! I sighed, my heart plunging to my knees. All I wanted was to go for a walk. Eventually, Dad got the hang of the harness and finally we were allowed to go outside.

Yes! I gasped, as we opened the front door. *At last!*

I was raring to go, but Dad was a little hesitant about being pulled along by me because, when I was on full power, it was like being dragged along by an out-of-control lawn mower, with me being the mower! Emma decided that we should walk to the community shop, where John bought his food. But as soon as we stepped inside the shop, I spotted lots of people; one of them was holding a TV camera. Dad apologised for butting in, and the people explained they were from the TV station. They were filming a news item about the shop, which was different to most because it was run by people from the village.

'Can we interview you?' the lady reporter asked Dad.

I pushed in between the two of them.

Hey, don't forget me! I cried.

The lady smiled and dipped down to stroke my back.

'Yes, if we could film you both, then that would be great!' she said.

Film star dog! I grinned. *Wait till I tell Kilty!*

But if I thought it'd be glamorous, I was wrong. Instead the woman asked Dad loads of boring questions about what the shop meant to him. My eyes glazed over as the voices droned on and on. I was just zoning out when I spotted something out of the corner of my eye: lots of big, old-fashioned sweetie jars lined up along the floor. I sneaked a look upwards – everyone was busy listening to Dad. As I inched closer to one of the jars, that's when I read the label: '*Strawberry Sweets*'.

Whoo hoo! Not only were they sweets, I'd just hit the strawberry jackpot! I wrapped a front paw around the neck of the jar and tried to twist the top off, but it was stuck. So I twisted a little harder, waiting for the lid to pop off.

Just a bit more force and it should come off... I huffed, dreaming of the sticky sweets inside.

'Dez!' Emma called, as everyone turned to look at me.

I froze as the camera continued to whir, capturing it all

on live TV. The whole nation had just watched me, red-pawed, with my hand on the sweetie jar.

Afterwards, as he packed away his stuff, the cameraman started to laugh.

'It was so funny, John! You were just saying what a good dog Dez was when I caught him walking into the back of the shop, trying to break into the sweets.'

'I think he's hungry,' someone called out.

'He's *always* hungry,' Dad replied. 'He's a greedy Labrador!'

I'd just become a TV star, but not for the right reasons. That afternoon, my mobile phone buzzed: it was Stan.

I saw you. We all did! Tut, tut! But sweets... and when you're on duty!

I blushed as I typed a reply.

I know, I was so embarrassed, but I think Dad's forgiven me.

That afternoon, Dad, Emma and I walked to his nieces' house.

'You're going to love Pippa and Sophie,' he told me. 'And I know they're going to love you too.'

As soon as we walked in through the door, two little girls came running over and smothered me with kisses.

Wow! Call this work! I shrieked, lapping up the attention.

Dad told them all about my botched attempt to steal strawberry sweets. I cringed as I listened because I knew it was wrong – stealing *was* wrong. But thankfully, they just laughed about it.

As we sat there, Dad explained that it had been Pippa, the eldest of the two, who had changed his life. She phoned him one day when he was really fed up and that's when he decided to get a guide dog.

'When I first lost my sight, I spoke to Pippa, who made me realise that just because I couldn't see, it didn't mean my life was over. So it's down to her that we met, Dez. If it hadn't been for Pippa, none of this would have happened.'

I gazed lovingly at Pippa and Sophie. Dad was right – they were very special little girls indeed. It wasn't just Dad who owed them everything, I did too. But it also made me worry about the future. *If I didn't pass the walking exam with Dad, it would all be over and then I'd be sent away. I couldn't even bring back a simple toy. Who'd want a guide dog who walked too fast and stole sweets? No one, that's who,* I thought.

So that's why I had to pass my final test. If I didn't, Dad would have to start again with another dog, and then I'd lose my dad and my new best friend forever.

CHAPTER 16

GUIDE DOG EXAMS

*D*eep *breath, don't forget to take a deep breath,* I reminded myself as I puffed and panted on the pavement. This was our make-or-break moment – my final guide dog exam.

Pass this, and you'll stay with Dad for life. Fail, and then who knows where you'll end up?

As I stretched out my paws and shook them to try and loosen myself up, I was getting ready, preparing myself for the biggest test of my life. Everything else had been puppy play up until this moment.

'Now just relax,' Emma told us both. 'Relax and try your best, and whatever you do, John, just go with Dez. Trust your dog.'

I gulped nervously.

No pressure there, then!

'Right,' said Emma, taking a step back.

She stood to the side with a man called Alun, who would

be marking us, but more importantly, he was the man who would decide our fate.

My belly rumbled as I tried to think of nice things to take my nerves away.

Strawberries. Strawberries and cream. Ice cream and monkey's blood. Jam doughnuts, strawberry shortcake, hmmm... My mouth began to drool.

'Dez,' said Emma, snapping me back into the moment. 'Right, John, whenever you're ready.'

As I tried to concentrate on the walk ahead, I felt Dad's hand trembling through the harness. I'd be leading Dad to his friends' house, a couple called Bob and Kath. I knew the route well because we'd practised it for weeks. In fact, I knew it like the back of my paw

But what if I put a paw wrong? What if I take a wrong turn?

I shook my head to try and rid the negative thought from my head. That wouldn't happen because we'd worked hard, and now I was ready. I tried my best to slow my legs down and not walk too fast, but Dad was great because, like me, he was a fast walker too – Emma had matched us well. We walked the route to perfection and we were almost there when I turned the final corner.

Oh no! I gasped.

Usually clear, the pavement had been blocked by some roadwork barriers, which had fallen over onto it.

There's no way Dad will be able to step over them. I panicked, my mind going blank. *Now, think! Remember what they taught you at Guide Dog School. Stay calm and think it through.*

So I took a deep breath; I knew what I had to do. As

we approached the obstruction, I realised Dad's natural instinct would be to carry straight on. If he had, then he would've fallen over the barriers blocking the path. Instead, I came to a sudden halt.

'Eh?' I heard Dad mumble because he knew we shouldn't stop there.

I turned towards the road and looked left, then right, watching all the time.

Go with me on this one, Dad, just trust me, I begged.

'Find your way, Dez,' he insisted, giving me the green light to make the right decision.

This was it.

Although he was wondering where on earth I was leading him, I knew Dad believed in me and that gave me the strength to carry on.

Left. Clear. Right. Clear. Left. Still clear. Right. Still clear, I muttered to myself, checking the road again for traffic until I knew it was safe to take Dad onto it. We wouldn't be crossing it, but walking up alongside the kerb and then back onto the pavement as soon as it was safe to do so. Although it was only a few precious steps, I knew I had to be extra-careful. Soon enough, we were back on the pavement, safe and sound, clear of the obstruction and only steps from Bob and Kath's front door.

We'd made it!

With the test at an end, Emma came rushing over to congratulate us.

'It was a gold badge moment – Dez was magnificent – you both were!'

I felt proud of both Dad and me because I knew we'd come such a long way in such a short space of time. Once home, Emma handed us our very own guide-dog harness. It was a symbol we'd done it. After she left, I nudged Dad's hand with my nose, lifted my head and urged him to put the harness on.

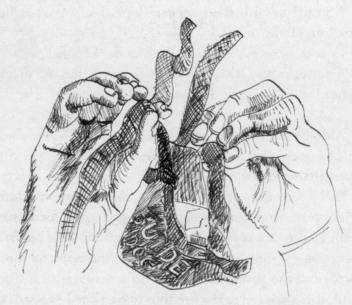

What are we waiting for? I said, dancing around.

'Come on then, why not?' Dad grinned, as we burst out through the front door and headed over to the community shop to share the good news.

Of course, everyone was delighted and before I knew it, we were the talk of the village. John and Dez, or Dez and John – we were a team and no one and nothing could ever part us!

CHAPTER 16

LOLLIPOP
THIEF

My reputation as a guide dog spread through the village until soon it was Valentine's Day and cards started falling through the letterbox. Dad preened himself, sat down and waited for a friend to read them out. But the smile was soon wiped off his face when his mate told him they were all addressed to ME!

See, I giggled, rolling on the floor, laughing. *Told you I'm better-looking than you!*

The shock on his face was priceless. It'd been the same when our birthdays arrived – I'd received so many cards that Dad put his next to mine so that he looked more popular.

'I have to admit, Dez, everybody loves you,' he laughed, tickling my ear.

I know, what can I say? I'm a superstar! I giggled.

But it was only a joke because I knew no one loved me more than Dad, and I felt exactly the same.

We had such a good life together. When we were out walking, I met loads of new friends, including Isla, a beautiful flat-coated black retriever. Her mum and dad were doctors, and they were good friends with John.

'So, you're a guide dog?' Isla began.

'Yes, that's right, I'm newly qualified,' I said, sticking my chest out proudly.

'Ooh, how exciting!' she squealed.

Isla and I became good friends, and I began to look forward to our walks because I knew I would get to spend time with her. It wasn't long before I'd fallen for Isla and we started going out together. Then I met Jangle, who belonged to a lovely woman called Monica, who worked for Guide Dogs.

'I've heard lots about you,' Jangle cooed, fluttering her eyelashes, and in that moment I was smitten again. I was just a hopeless romantic, and before I knew it I'd fallen for both of them. They were the same type of dog and equally lovely, but I couldn't choose between them, so I kept them a secret from one another.

Although they were supposed to be a secret, I received Valentine's cards from both Isla and Jangle, which was a little awkward. I'd also got more from Pippa and Sophie. I loved the girls especially because they'd asked their school to become involved in helping to raise more money for Guide Dogs, so John and I visited one day. We'd walked into Assembly and the whole school had been waiting to greet us, which was fantastic. The children vowed to raise as much money as they could for Guide Dogs to help pay for more dogs like me, and they did. It made me feel proud that I'd helped make a difference. Life was certainly on the up, so when Dad and I strolled through a shopping centre one afternoon I felt really happy. In fact, I was so happy, padding along, that for a split second, I almost forgot I was a guide dog because all I could see was a little girl heading towards me in her pushchair, holding a red-coloured lollipop.

Hmmm, strawberries, I sighed, my mouth watering at the thought.

As the girl came closer, she spotted me sniffing the air and held the lollipop out towards me.

For me? I asked. *Are you sure? Don't you want it yourself?*

But the toddler didn't answer; instead, she stuck the lolly right underneath my nose as we walked by.

Well, it'd be rude not to, I thought as I opened my mouth and plucked the lolly from her hand.

Dad and me had only walked a minute or so longer when I heard a piercing cry: the toddler had changed her mind and now she wanted her lolly back! I dipped my head down as she pointed over at me, glad that Dad hadn't seen what I'd done. Instead, my paws picked up pace as I tried to lead him towards the exit.

'Excuse me...' the little girl's mother said, running after us.

'Yes?' Dad replied, stopping to turn around.

'I'm sorry to bother you, but your dog has got, er, well, he's got a lollipop sticking out of his mouth.'

I bowed my head in shame and tried to hide the lolly stick, but the strawberry tasted so delicious I couldn't help but suck it. I knew once more I was letting my belly rule my head, only this time I didn't care. It was *my* lolly, and I didn't want to let it go!

SLURP!

'*What?*' gasped Dad.

'Your dog,' she said, beginning to giggle, 'erm... it's your dog, he's... he's got a lollipop in his mouth. Oh, he does look funny!' She smirked, before dissolving into fits of laughter.

By now, people had stopped to stare. A circle had gathered round to point and stare at me, the dog with the lolly. Dad put his hand down and ran his fingers along the edge of my velvety mouth until he'd located the lolly stick. Grabbing hold of it, he started tugging to try and pull it out of my mouth, but it tasted so delicious that I didn't want to let go.

No, It's mine! I whimpered. *The little girl gave it to me; she's just changed her mind, honestly!*

'I can smell it now, I should have known!' Dad gasped in despair. 'It's strawberry flavour too – it's his favourite. Come on, Dez, give it back!'

Nope! I decided, wrapping my tongue around it, giving it an almighty slurp. *I haven't stolen it – it was a present, so you can't have it. It's mine!*

It soon became a lollipop tug of war but eventually, after a little tussle, Dad finally pulled the lolly out of the front of my mouth.

PLOP! It sounded as my lips smacked together.

Hey, I was enjoying that, spoilsport! I huffed.

'*Dez!*' Dad scolded, his voice so serious that I looked down guiltily.

Uh-oh, I'm in trouble – again!

The woman explained how her little girl had waved the lolly in front of my nose. She wasn't angry because she thought it was funny.

'I'm always telling her not to wave sweets about, but you know what kids are like.' She laughed.

Dad huffed. 'Yes, I know – I'm standing with a big kid on a lead right now,' he said, nudging against me.

Dad put his hand in his pocket and gave the woman a pound so that she could buy her daughter lots more lollies. She tried to hand it back, but he refused.

'No, please, take it.'

165

Then he tugged on the lead and told me to go forward.

'A guide dog and a lollipop thief...' he muttered, as we walked on. It made me feel even worse. 'But sweets, and when you're on duty...'

I wanted to argue that I hadn't stolen it because the little girl had given it to me, but I knew he was right and I was wrong.

Sorry, Dad! I whimpered, but he wasn't interested because he was so disappointed.

'Home!' he ordered.

That's when I knew it, and not for the first time, my sweet tooth had got me in trouble.

CHAPTER 18

SUPERMARKETS, SCHOOLS AND SWIMMING POOLS

Although he was a little bit miffed with me for taking the lollipop, Dad didn't stay cross for long. Instead, he volunteered us to take part in some major fundraising for Guide Dogs. So we met up with Monica and Diana, two fundraisers for the charity. I'd met them before and loved them both, especially Monica's dog, Jangle, my other 'secret' girlfriend. A retired guide dog, who lived with Monica, Jangle was not only beautiful, but wise too. As we strolled in the park, Jangle turned to me: she had something to say.

'Someone thought they'd seen you and me walking together last week, but I told them it couldn't be me because I was out fundraising,' she began.

I gulped down a nervous breath – I'd just been rumbled.

'Erm, really?' I said. My face blushed because I realised she was referring to my recent walk with Isla. 'They must've been mistaken. It can't have been me. I've been busy... and...' I stammered.

'It *was* you, because they recognised John,' she insisted.

GULP!

I held a paw up to my mouth, desperately trying to think of a good excuse. It was hard being in love with two women.

'Now, let me think. Yes, I did bump into another black retriever. Come to think of it, yes, I suppose she does look a little bit like you, though obviously not as beautiful.'

Jangle dipped her head and blushed slightly.

'You'd charm the birds out of the trees, Dezzy boy, do you know that?' She smirked. 'But listen, there's something I need to tell you.'

'What's that?' I asked, relieved she'd changed the subject.

'We desperately need to raise funds for Guide Dogs. If we don't, then there'll be lots of people like John, who won't be able to have a dog,' Jangle explained.

'What? You mean there'll be people like Dad, who won't be given a dog?' I gasped.

Jangle nodded sadly. 'It's money, Dez. It costs a fortune to train a dog like you, and Guide Dogs is a charity, so it relies on the public to help support it and keep it going.'

'But if we don't raise enough money, then we won't be able to train more dogs. What happens then?'

Jangle stopped in her tracks and looked me directly in the eye. 'I don't know. That's why we need people to help raise money, and as a guide dog, it's pretty much your duty, Dez.'

She was right, and the thought of Guide Dogs not being able to train more pups horrified me.

'But how do I do it? I mean, what do I do?'

'You just have to smile and be polite,' Jangle explained. (She'd been to lots of fundraising events with Monica so she was an old hand, or paw, at that sort of thing.)

'But what if people don't like me? What if they don't give us any money?'

Jangle stifled a giggle. '*What?* With a cute little face like that?' She smiled, brushing my cheek with her paw. 'Who could resist?'

And Jangle was right: as soon as people saw Dad and me standing in the foyer of the local supermarket with a collection tin, they came over. Not everyone was friendly, because some people were in a rush, but I tried to catch the eye of every single person because I needed to help raise vital funds to train more dogs.

'Hello,' a woman said, smiling as she stroked me.

'Hello,' John replied.

I looked up at him.

Daaad, she's talking to me, not you! I whined, standing up.

'What a beautiful dog! What's his name?' she asked, turning her attention back towards Dad.

'He's called Dez and he's my lifesaver.'

I sat as Dad explained how

169

he'd lost his eyesight but how I'd come along and changed his life for the better. The woman listened and when he'd finished, she dropped loads of pound coins into our collection tin.

Well done, Dad, we're one step closer to funding another dog like me!

Moments later, a young mum spoke to us.

'I just had to come over and say hello. It's your dog – as soon as I walked in, he looked straight at me. Is it okay if my son strokes him?'

Course it is, I said, jumping to my feet. *The more strokes, the better!*

Afterwards, she put even more coins in our tin.

This is easy! I thought happily.

We needed to raise money because Jangle had explained that it costs Guide Dogs £400 a week to train a dog like me. Sadly, money doesn't grow on trees, and I was worried that without fundraisers like Monica, Diana, and Jangle, there'd be lots more Johns, sad and alone. Raising money was a huge job because it costs £50,000 to fund one guide dog throughout its life. I knew Dad and I wouldn't be able to raise that much, but the thought we were raising something made me feel good.

'We're doing really well, Dezzy boy,' he said, patting me on the head.

I know, I'm the one doing all the hard work! I grinned as I continued to eyeball every person who came through the door.

By the time we'd finished, our collection tin was full and

we were both shattered. Still, Dad volunteered us to do more fundraising, but I didn't mind because I loved all the attention.

One day, we were raising money in another supermarket when an elderly lady wandered over towards us.

'Excuse me, would it be okay to give your dog a treat?' she enquired.

Treat! My ears pricked up as soon as I heard it. I scrambled onto all fours eagerly, but the lady explained she had to go into the supermarket first to buy it. My face drooped in disappointment. For the next hour, I watched and waited for her to reappear. When she finally did so, I bounced up onto all four paws and started to dance in circles.

Treat, treat, treat! I panted.

I watched as she handed a packet to Dad and walked away. But he was unable to see what she'd given him, so he called after her to ask what it was.

'Oh, it's a Twix,' she replied.

I watched as the expression on his face changed from one of delight to disappointment. But I was truly shocked when I saw him slide the chocolate bar sneakily into the top pocket of his jacket. I looked up, my eyes boring into his, willing him to give it to me.

'No, you can't have it mate,' he insisted. 'It's chocolate, it could kill you!'

I huffed and slumped back down on the floor.

Spoilsport!

But Dad was right: dogs aren't allowed chocolate and for a very good reason, which is that we can die from it, even

I knew that. It was hard letting the chocolate go, but when I thought about what it could do to me, for once I lost my appetite.

Following our success in supermarkets, we started visiting workplaces and then schools. I loved going into schools because the children would cuddle and smother me with kisses. Also, I wanted to teach them how important guide dogs are and also the job we do, changing peoples' lives every single day.

One day, Dad was sitting in a primary school talking to a group of children, who were covering him in 'Transformer' stickers. I tried not to laugh – he looked so funny with his 'Transformers' jacket.

'It's okay to stroke and cuddle a guide dog when he's not working,' he told the children, 'but you must never distract one when he's working because he needs to concentrate at all times.'

'Is Dez off-duty now?' a little boy asked.

'He is.' John grinned.

Within seconds, I was surrounded by a dozen children all wanting to kiss me and stroke my fur. I was mobbed, but I lifted my head up in midst of the scrum to look at Dad.

This is the life! Call this work? I giggled. I loved my job so much.

Dad wanted to raise more money for Guide Dogs, so he decided to do a ten-mile sponsored swim.

You're joking me! I sniggered, trying my best not to laugh. I loved Dad, but he was hardly an athlete. But true to his word, he went to the local leisure centre to train for the big swim.

Can I come? Can I come? I barked, dancing around his feet as he grabbed a towel and put it in a bag.

'You can, but dogs aren't allowed in the water, so you'll have to wait in reception for me.'

Spoilsport!

But there were benefits. For starters, I got to sit behind the front desk with the lady who sold the tickets, which made me feel very important. I also got loads of free hugs. But as soon as I heard Dad come out through the changing-room door, I jumped up and scrambled over the top of the counter.

I've missed you so much, Dad. I've missed yoooouuu! I whined.

'Aw, you daft thing!' he laughed, putting the harness over my head.

As we walked home I gazed up at him adoringly.

'Blimey, that swimming was hard work, Dezzy boy!' he remarked.

Ha! Told you you're not an athlete! I sniggered.

Dad trained hard until soon he'd managed to swim all ten miles. The people in the community shop and others online donated money. Soon, he'd not only reached his target, he'd doubled it – raising well over £1,000 for Guide Dogs. I was so proud of him!

A few days later, we visited an infant school. I was mobbed as usual, but then something extraordinary happened.

'Bye-bye, Doggy,' a little girl aged five years old called out. She stretched out her hand to touch my fur, so I nuzzled in against her.

'Do you want to meet Dez?' Dad asked.

The little girl didn't reply but her teacher did.

'I can't believe it,' she gasped. 'This is the first time we've ever heard her speak! It's your dog,' she said, looking down at me, 'she's besotted by him.'

I lifted my head because in that moment I felt proud. Proud, because I'd not only helped Dad get his life back, but the little girl too. I was proud because we'd helped raise lots of money to pay for more dogs like me. Between us, and the other fundraisers up and down the country, both human and canine, we'd helped raise thousands of pounds for Guide Dogs so that it could carry on its vital work. It made me feel good that Dad and I had made a difference, no matter how small that'd been. But most of all, I felt proud to be a guide dog, because for a dog, it's the most important job in the whole wide world!

CHAPTER 19

BISCUITS, CAKE AND BELLYACHE

Although I'd played my part and had helped with lots of fundraising, I still had a sweet tooth and I craved sweets almost every day. Sometimes I'd fall asleep and dream about them. I'd have brilliant dreams where strawberries the size of houses would chase people down the street. I'd step forward, like a superdog, and save them all by gobbling the giant fruit down in one go. I loved anything strawberry but guide dogs have to follow a strict diet. Although the people at Guide Dogs thought I did stick to one myself, I'd started to get a little fat because I'd snuffle treats whenever Dad was busy.

Soon it was Christmas, our first together, and I couldn't wait to give Dad his present – a new toy for him to throw for me!

'You've been a good boy, Dez,' he insisted. 'Santa will bring you lots of goodies.'

Eeekkk! I squealed. I could hardly wait. That night, as he tucked me up in bed, I couldn't sleep because I wanted it to be Christmas Day.

'Get some rest, Dez,' said Dad, patting me on the head, 'because Father Christmas won't come if you stay awake.'

So I screwed my Labrador eyes up tight, because I wanted to sleep. I didn't want to let any of the surprise sneak beneath my eyelids. The following morning, I woke with a start.

Christmas! It's Christmas! I cried, thumping Dad's bedroom door open with a loud bang.

'Blimey, Dez! I wondered what it was!' he chuckled, pulling on his dressing gown. 'Has Santa been?'

Santa's been, Santa's been, Santa's been... I whimpered, nudging him to hurry up, so I could open up my presents.

'Okay, okay, I'm coming!' he said, holding out his hands.

Dad had bought me loads of presents, including a big, juicy bone, which tasted delicious. I'd wished for a strawberry one, but he explained they weren't very good for me. When I'd finally ripped all the wrapping paper to shreds, he got to his feet.

'Come on, Dez,' he said, grabbing the harness, 'let's go for a walk.'

Yipeee! I shouted. *This WAS the best day of my life!*

He took me to the park, which was pretty much deserted apart from a few children on new bikes and scooters, and people trying to walk off the heavy Christmas food they

had been gobbling down. Dad undid my lead and off I ran, like a maniac, around the park. As I ran, I noticed that Dad had sat down on a park bench. With him safe, I decided to go and explore. I was just wandering along the path when I spotted something red poking out through the long grass. I sniffed the air.

Strawberries! My mouth drooled.

Checking over my shoulder, I sneaked closer and stuck out a paw to part the grass and uncover the treasure. I gasped – it was a pack of Jammie Dodgers!

Bingo! I grinned. *Biscuits and strawberry jam, I'd just hit the jackpot!*

What Dad doesn't know, won't hurt him, I thought, as I proceeded to munch my way through the whole packet. Afterwards, I felt a little sick and my belly was stuffed. But it *was* Christmas day, and I had been a good boy.

'Where have you been?' Dad asked suspiciously when I returned.

Nowhere, I lied, dipping my head.

We walked back home. It was only a short walk, but by the end of it, I felt decidedly green about the gills. Then I burped loudly.

BURP!

Dad, I whimpered, *I feel a bit sick...*

He had guessed something was wrong because I whined as sickness gripped me.

'Dez, are you alright?'

No, poorly. Need a doctor...

He picked up the phone and rang the vet. I could tell he was worried, which worried me even more.

'I'm so sorry, Dad,' I wailed, over and over.

But it was Christmas Day, so someone had to come out and take me away. I was so upset that I cried all the way there because my poor dad was all alone now. The whole night I cried because I realised just how stupid I'd been. This time my belly was in real trouble and to make matters worse, it was all my fault!

I'm sorry! I promise I'll never eat a whole packet of Jammie Dodgers again.

The following day, after a good night's sleep and some special medicine, I began to feel better, so the veterinary nurse took me home.

'Dez!' Dad called, bending down to give me a hug.

Oooh, not too hard! I moaned. *I've still got bellyache...*

I sounded just like Vinnie, but I couldn't help it – I felt as sick as a dog! In the end, Dad sat up with me for three days solid, trying to nurse me back to health. He even dug out my special blankie and Mr Roo Roo to cheer me up.

Don't tell anyone, you know, about the teddy, I begged.

I'd actually started to feel better the next day, although I didn't tell Dad because I loved all the attention. Eventually, though, he sussed me out.

'Er, I think you're okay,' he decided, as I leapt off him a little too quickly, one dinner time. 'So I reckon we need to get back to work.'

Okay, I agreed, *and I promise I'll never, ever touch cake or biscuits again.*

But my promise didn't last long, because I let my stomach rule my head one more time.

A few weeks later, Dad was asked to give a speech to around 200 people at a posh event to raise money for Guide Dogs. Of course, it was mostly about me so I got to go along too.

'Guide Dogs are remarkable,' he told the audience. 'Take Dez, here,' he said, pointing down at me. I lifted my head to acknowledge my fans. 'He's so intelligent and so well-behaved.'

Oh, honestly, it's nothing! I blushed, as Dad proceeded to tell everyone how fantastic I was. By the time he'd finished, the audience were on their feet, clapping. I'm not sure if the fame went to my head, but as we left the stage I noticed something: a huge, chocolate cake filled with strawberries.

Hmmmm, I drooled, my tongue licking my lips in anticipation. I was supposed to be watching Dad, but now I couldn't take my eyes off that cake.

It looks sooooo good... I sighed dreamily, as my belly rumbled.

Just then a lady stepped forward to help Dad down the steps.

'No, I'm fine, honestly,' he insisted, but she grabbed his arm.

With the harness free, I ran at full pelt across the room towards the table and the cake.

Strawberries! I howled.

The cake got bigger and bigger as I bounded towards it.

Hundreds of pairs of eyes watched as I leapt up onto the table and snatched the biggest slice I could sink my doggy teeth into.

'DEZ!' Dad shouted, trying to pull the chocolate cake from my mouth. The woman had snitched on me, telling him what I'd done, as the whole room roared with laughter. The well-behaved guide dog – the star of the show – had only gone and nicked the biggest slice of chocolate cake in the room!

Although Dad had dashed over and tried to seize the cake from my mouth, I'd already gobbled it up.

'NOM, NOM, NOM...'

I noticed Dad had blushed bright red.

'Talk about showing me up, in front of everyone, too!'

Sorry, Dad, I whimpered.

But I wasn't, not really, because the cake – or rather the strawberries – had tasted delicious!

CHAPTER 20

GUIDE DOG
OF THE YEAR

'So, I heard about the cake,' said Stan (he'd called me up on my mobile for a chat).

'*Don't!*' I cringed. 'I'm still in the doghouse for that!'

'Oh Dez, when will you ever learn? Dogs and sweet things just don't mix!'

'I know,' I whined. 'But the thing is, I've got a really sweet tooth – I can't help it.'

Stan sighed. 'I know, son. You're such a brilliant guide dog, one of the best, but the thing is, you need to learn how to act like one, and whatever you do, stop stealing sweet things!'

I knew he was right: if I wanted to do well, then I had to change my ways. So I decided to try my very best. Whenever I saw a sticky boiled sweet stuck to the pavement, even though I wanted to wolf it down, I told myself 'no'. When the ice-cream van drove past our flat, I clamped both paws against my ears and hummed to drown out the noise.

I can beat this, I vowed.

Soon, I was trying so hard that everyone had noticed.

'You're a bit of a good boy all of a sudden,' Jangle said, grinning, as Monica and Dad walked us in the park.

'I know, I'm trying really hard to be good.'

'Is it because of the competition?'

'What competition?'

Jangle explained that every year, Guide Dogs held a competition to find the very best guide dogs in the country.

'I thought that's what you were trying to do, win something.'

But I shook my head. 'I didn't know anything about it. Why, does Dad know?'

Jangle shrugged. 'Nope, I don't think so, but my mum does.'

Afterwards I thought about the competition all the time because I knew just how proud Mum and Niki would be. I tried to imagine the look on Emma's face if I won an award. I wanted to win one, but not for myself: I wanted to win one for Emma and Dad. If it hadn't been for Emma, I'd probably still be stuck at Guide Dog School, waiting to be chosen, and if it wasn't for Dad... well, I shuddered as an icy-cold blast shot down my spine because I couldn't imagine life without Dad – he meant the whole world to me. After my conversation with Jangle, I did everything I could to get nominated for an award. Every walk we went on, I followed all the guide dog rules. A few months later, Monica knocked at the door: she had some news.

'John, you and Dez have been nominated for a Life Changing Award at the Guide Dog of the Year Awards ceremony in London,' Monica told us.

'What? No way!' Dad gasped.

I grinned because I was thrilled. Finally, they'd noticed all the hard work I'd been putting in.

'Are you sure?' Dad asked.

'Well, I should be because I'm the one who's nominated you,' Monica confessed.

My jaw dropped open as I looked at Jangle. 'Did you have anything to do with this?'

Jangle's head dipped down. 'I might have had a quick word with Mum. But Dez, you and John have done this yourselves – you're brilliant together. Anyone who knows or meets you can tell that.'

'Is it that obvious? I thought I was the only one who'd noticed.'

Jangle shook her head. 'No, not at all! In fact, Mum and Emma said you and John are a match made in Heaven.'

'Did they?' I whimpered.

I so wanted Emma and Monica to be proud of me.

Only Monica wasn't finished. 'But John, I nominated you and I'm pleased to say you've won!'

Now it was Dad's turn to stand there with his mouth open.

'I can't believe it!' he gasped.

Monica explained that now we needed to get ready

because we had to travel to a big, swanky awards ceremony in London.

'What on earth will I wear, Dez?' Dad asked later, as he sorted through the bottom of his wardrobe.

Hey, I wouldn't worry about that, I woofed, staring at my reflection. I held out my paw and smoothed down my fringe... *because I'm going to be star of the show!*

On the evening itself, I felt really nervous as we were called up onto the stage to accept our award from a man off the TV. I was so nervous that somehow I tripped up, which made Dad falter for a second. To make matters worse, I felt his hand tremble as he clutched the harness and instantly I knew that he was as scared as I was. Soon we were standing there in front of a huge crowd, with everyone looking at us. When I thought about this, I took a deep gulp. I had thought it would be great up on stage, but now we were there I felt really, really scared. In fact, I couldn't wait to get off! Once we'd been given our award we turned to leave, but were stopped by one of the organisers, who told us to stay exactly where we were.

'Each winner from each of the different categories is automatically nominated for the main award of the evening,' she explained to Dad.

'Er, and what's that?' he asked.

I budged in closer to hear.

'It's for Guide Dog of the Year.'

Dad's hand trembled as I gulped with nerves.

Nobody had said anything about a second award! I panicked as my legs began to shake.

Dad and I trembled like a pair of jellies on a plate as we waited for the winner to be announced. I looked around at the other dogs standing there and recognised a few from my training days. They were all brilliant guide dogs, and so much better than I was. It made me feel even worse and I wondered what on earth I was doing standing up on stage. My mind whirred and soon I felt quite dizzy with it all. It was hot underneath the spotlights and the posh new collar around my neck felt a little tight. We hadn't won, so I felt a bit of a twit standing there... Suddenly the TV man began to speak.

'And the winner is...' he said, pausing for dramatic effect.

As I looked over towards the exit, I wanted to get off the stage because my legs were aching from all that standing and I was worried Dad was tired too.

'...and the winner is Dez!'

Eh? Hang on, I mumbled.

I looked around but everyone was on their feet, looking at us as the room erupted with thunderous applause.

For a minute there, I thought he said my name... Dez!

'Well done, Dezzy boy!' said Dad, his voice croaking with emotion. He dipped down a hand and gently patted me on my back.

What? You mean, I won? I really did?

I looked out at the crowd to try and find Monica and Jangle. It didn't take long because they were standing there, crying with joy.

Whoo hoo! Go for it, Dez! Jangle cried, as she punched the air with her front paw.

'That's my boy!' Monica wept proudly.

I was so stunned that I couldn't take it in, but then Dad was handed a microphone and started to speak. He thanked everyone, especially Emma.

'Without Emma, we wouldn't be here today,' Dad explained.

I nodded because it was true. Without Emma, or all the brilliant people at Guide Dogs, none of this would have happened. Afterwards, we were swamped by reporters and photographers, all wanting to speak to us and take our photos. Just then, the man off the TV stepped forward and handed me a giant biscuit bone.

'Dez, can you look up at the camera, please?' a photographer called.

But I was too busy eating my first prize.

'NOM, NOM, NOM...'

Everyone laughed. Afterwards, we had lots of photographs taken together. I couldn't believe people wanted to take a photograph of me, Dezzy boy. One of the proudest moments of my life, it didn't feel as good as qualifying as a guide dog but it certainly came a close second! The following day, we were still so excited that Dad called in at the shop to tell all our friends, who were as thrilled as we were. As we closed the shop door behind us, Dad turned to me.

'There's just one more surprise left,' he grinned.

What could it be? I wondered. *Perhaps it was a new toy or a big juicy bone?*

The flat seemed dark and empty as we approached it. Dad put the key in the lock, but as soon as he pushed open the front door, there was an enormous cheer! I stood there, my mouth hanging open, because it was full of my pals. Stan and Willow were standing in the corner with Bonnie and Kilty, who was holding a 'Welcome Home' balloon between her teeth. Max was running around the room, screaming with excitement, while Marvellous Meg looked at him, shaking her head.

'SURPRISE!' the gang called.

Is this for me, Dad? All for me? I asked, my tail wagging in the air. But that wasn't all. As I turned, I spotted Mum, Vesper, Vicky, Vinnie and Violet all waiting to hug me.

'I'm so proud of you, Dez,' Mum sobbed. 'My boy, Guide Dog of the Year! I always told you that you were special,' she said, slurping the top of my head with a big, wet kiss.

189

'Well done, bruv!'

I felt a tap on my shoulder and turned: it was Violet. She stepped forward and wrapped both paws around me.

'Wait, leave some for me!' Vicky laughed, as she pushed her out of the way to grab me too.

'Ooh, I'm so proud, I could burst!' she wept, making my shoulder damp with her tears. Vinnie peeled her off and pulled me into a big hug.

'But what about germs?' I asked.

'Oh, forget that!' he said, with

190

a wave of his paw. 'It's not every day your brother wins Guide Dog of the Year, is it?'

I shut my eyes and let him hug me. When I opened them, I saw Star standing behind him.

'Told you, I knew you could do it!' she said, taking a step forward. 'I'm so proud of you, Dez. See, it doesn't matter what shape, size or colour you are, if you're good and you try your best then you'll always win!'

'Come here,' I said, kissing her on the cheek.

Just then the door to the kitchen opened and out came Niki, my puppy-walker mum, followed by her family, Jon, Molly, Harry and Sam.

'We're so proud of you!' Niki said, smothering me in kisses.

As I cuddled Molly and the boys, Max held his paws up in front of his face and made the sound of a trumpet. Seconds later, Winston walked out of the kitchen with a huge strawberry-shaped cake strapped to his back.

'Now then, me old china plate, I hopes you're gonna make a wish,' he said, winking at me.

Niki carefully undid the cake and placed it down on the floor.

'But there's no candle,' I mumbled.

Without warning, the cake exploded as two paws and a head shot out through the top of it.

'Ta dah!' a little voice cried out as a Yorkshire terrier zoomed into view.

'*Roger!*' I gasped. Then I shook my head – he was wearing a long pink coloured evening gown.

'SURPRISE!' everyone shouted.

'Brilliant!' Roger gasped, tiptoeing out of the remnants of the sticky cake. 'Isn't it wonderful?' he said, staring up at me. 'What, the cake?'

'No, the dress!' he said, with a wide smile. I was shocked because I'd never seen Roger smile before. 'It's the dress... Look, it's ruined!' He threw his head back with laughter, stepped out of the cake, pulled down the dress and kicked it to one side.

'That's better! Now then, I thought there was meant to be a paaarrrrty!'

Max jumped to his feet and raced over towards Dad's CD player. He pressed 'play' as 'House of Fun', a song by a group called Madness, boomed through the speakers. Dad grinned because it was his favourite band.

'Oh, I love this one!' Max hollered above the music as he turned it up to full volume. 'I love Madness because they're a little bit crrrrraaazy, like me!' He jumped and bounced around the room on two back legs. 'Come on, Meg!' he cried, pulling her onto the dance floor.

Soon everyone had joined in. Dogs danced, barked and woofed with delight as Kilty howled above them all, singing out of tune along with the music.

'Eeee, I hope that Simon Cowell's listening, pet!' she shouted to me across the room.

'Is she always that bad at singing?' Dad asked, putting his fingers inside his ears, 'because she's making a right old racket!'

I nodded my head and gazed up at him. As I watched both humans and dogs dance in time to the music, I rested my chin upon his lap. With all my friends and family there, and with Dad by my side, I knew life simply couldn't get any better. I'd thought becoming a guide dog had been the best moment ever, but I'd been wrong, because today simply was the best day of my life!

THANK YOU

I love my life working as a guide dog and being a best pal to John, but there are so many people and dogs I'd like to thank that I really don't know where to start, so I'll start with one of the most important people – Emma Yard. Thank you, Emma, for not only choosing and believing in me, but also for helping to train me and ultimately, for matching me with John, who, thankfully, is as crackers as I am! I'm also grateful to Yvonne and Simon Dutton, my grandparents and boarders, Monica Cave and her husband Roger, and Diana Mager from Guide Dogs. My huge gratitude to John's nieces, Pippa and Sophie, who not only love and support me, they've also raised loads of money at school for Guide Dogs to pay for lots more pups like me. Well done, girls! Lots of love also to Niki, Jon, Sam, Harry and Molly for being the best puppy walkers in the world!

As for my canine pals, a big thank you goes to my best

friend Stan, who not only introduced me to park life, but ultimately taught me how to be a better dog too. Thank you to all my doggy pals: Misty, Bonnie, Kilty, Winston, Maxwell, Marvellous Meg, Willow, and, of course, Roger, and also my puppy family for their continued love and support. Special thanks go to Jangle, who as a retired guide dog knows just how important our work is. Every single day Guide Dogs change the lives of blind and partially sighted people. We not only give them freedom to live their lives, we're also their eyes on the world and their all-round best friends.

There are a few other people I would like to thank who have helped in the writing of this book, namely my avid proofreaders, Rebecca Wordsworth, and Cal and Isabella Ramsay.

Finally, the biggest credit has to go to my new dad, John Tovey. He not only walks and feeds me (though, sadly, not strawberries!), he is my favourite two-legged pal and constant companion. I'd be lost without him because he's my workmate, Dad and best friend, all rolled into one. I'm a very lucky pup indeed because somehow, and against all the odds, I ended up with the best owner in the world!

PLEASE HELP

I'm donating all my profits from this book to the Guide Dogs charity because every single day it changes the lives of people. It costs the Guide Dogs a whopping £50,000 to train and care for one guide dog from birth right through to its retirement. A massive £33,000 of this is spent on breeding and training a puppy like me. Guide Dogs rely entirely on donations. If you or your school would like to help pay for more dogs like me, please contact www. guidedogs.org.uk

To sponsor or name a puppy, please call: 0870 2406993.

Thank you,
Dez and John